THE PROGRESS AGENT HANDBOOK FOR INFLUENCE & CONNECTION

THE PROGRESS AGENT HANDBOOK FOR INFLUENCE & CONNECTION

Published by ***World Gumbo Publishing***

 Insight from Dean Lindsay's books, Cracking the Networking CODE and The Progress Challenge were utilized as source material for this book.

First Edition 2019

ISBN-13: 978-0-9761141-5-4

For more information, please call: **214-457-5656**
Email Dean Lindsay at: **Dean@DeanLindsay.com**
DeanLindsay.com

Contents

Cover Design: Jose Cordova
Photo Credit: Tammy Cromer

This book is dedicated to my Loves: Lena, Sofia & Ella.

Progress Agent Handbook Guarantee

When you - and your team - consistently utilize the concepts, insights, strategies and tips found in this Progress Agent Handbook:

- ✓ **You WILL Develop Greater Influence.**
- ✓ **You WILL Grow Stronger Connections.**
- ✓ **You WILL Prospect More Effectively and Win More Sales.**
- ✓ **You WILL Rock the Customer Experience & Earn Customer Loyalty.**
- ✓ **You WILL Attract More Quality Referrals and Recruits.**
- ✓ **You WILL Help Create a More Positive & Proactive Work Culture.**

This is guaranteed, ***but first*** you must ***act*** on the stuff in here. Learning **'HOW'** to become more influential and build powerful connections *is* ***NOT the goal.***

Actually, ***BECOMING more influential and building powerful business connections IS the goal.***

Learning should not lead to simply knowing. Learning should lead to ACTION.

Change is inevitable,
Progress is a choice.

INFLUENCE

in·flu·ence

1. the capacity to have an effect on the character, development, or behavior of someone or something, or
2. the power to shape policy or ensure favorable treatment from someone, especially through status, contacts, or wealth.
3. a person or thing with the capacity or power to have an effect on someone or something.

To Change Is Human; to Progress, Divine.

To increase our influence and make stronger connections we need to help others succeed, help them feel heard, feel cared for and important. In other words, we need to help others progress, and not merely change.

Change happens. We can't avoid change.

Lives evolve
Companies merge.
Markets bear and bull.
Organizations come together.
New technologies are created.
Children are born.
Tides turn.
Rain falls.

We are always in some form of transition, always arriving at some new *place* and dealing with new rollouts, new ideas, new everything. The very molecules inside the cells of our bodies are in constant flux. Our world and our lives are always changing, but they are not always progressing. **It is natural to resist what we view as change. However, we embrace what we view as progress.**

Progress means: forward movement, advance, gradual betterment. It takes awareness, character, discipline, and effort to progress.

Change is inevitable. Progress is a choice.

Everyone connects with the goal of progressing in some way. To grow our influence and connections, we need to be seen as an agent for their progress, a catalyst for them taking a positive next step forward. They need to feel that we make a positive impact in and on their life.

The PROGRESS PRINCIPLE:
Everything WE do, consciously or subconsciously, we do because we believe the perceived consequences of those actions will be us feeling some unique right mixture of the ***Six Ps of Progress.***

Pleasure
Peace of Mind
Profit
Prestige
Pain Avoidance
Power

This goes for eating, shopping, exercising, hugging, crying, working, going to the movies – whatever.

Each of us makes decisions on what to read, who to talk to, what to buy, where to eat, what to eat, who to take phone calls from, and who to help, based on whether we think these acts will bring us these six *influential* ***Six Ps of Progress.***

At a mostly subconscious level, we are continuously thinking to ourselves:

Will doing this action help me move toward pleasure, peace of mind, profit, prestige, power, or will it help me to avoid pain?

At each moment, we make decisions based on what we *think* will bring these benefits – short-term or long-term. It has long been the first principle of marketing to answer this unasked question.

To create powerful connections, we need to constantly be looking for ways to help others progress.

We must be seen as a catalyst in their progress, an agent for their progress. We need to be seen as *Progress Agents.*

We need to Be Progress in their eyes.

When you meet new people *- and with everyone you know* - make your number-one priority finding a way to help that person move toward the six Ps of Progress.

Marketing and advertising professionals – *totally dedicated to Influence and Connection* - know about the *Six Ps of Progress* (*though they don't call them that…yet).* Every ***effective*** business impression and every ***influential*** piece of marketing comes down to showing how a particular product or service can help the buyer progress toward feeling some unique mixture of ***pleasure, peace of mind, profit, prestige, and power, while also limiting or avoiding pain.***

We choose from an endless list of possible actions in order to try and achieve our desired outcomes, thereby feeling the *Six Ps of Progress.*
Some of these actions might include:

- *Volunteering at a food bank*
- *Dealing with an upset customer*
- *Cleaning out the garage*
- *Making sales calls*
- *Reading to our kids*
- *Praying*
- *Paying our taxes*
- *Sleeping*
- *Reach Out*
- *Watching a movie*
- *Writing this book*
- *Hanging out on Facebook*
- *Connecting*
- *Hiring a new employee*
- *Again, WHATEVER*

Each of these actions has positive meaning only when we believe it will help us feel a mixture of the Six Ps of Progress.

Though, we are all motivated by self-interest that does not have to be selfish thinking. When our desired outcome is for someone else to feel pleasure or avoid pain, this too is connected to us feeling an empathetic mixture of pleasure, peace of mind, profit, prestige, power, and pain avoidance. If it weren't, we wouldn't act. We give not so much out of the goodness of our hearts as for the goodness we feel in our hearts when we give.

The most important thing to carry with you is your reason why.

Most of us know that giving adds great pleasure to life and that a life of serving others also offers great influence and connections. In fact, as we begin to understand this, we see how the biggest givers end up with the most.

> **"You can have everything in life you want, if you will just help other people get what they want."**
>
> *-- Zig Ziglar*
>
> *(one of my all-time favorite quotes)*

A major hurdle to making great connections and *being progress* for ourselves and others is that nothing actually <u>causes</u> someone to feel the *Six Ps of Progress.* People, products, services, ideas, and companies can *offer* pleasure, peace of mind, profit, prestige, pain avoidance, and power. But they do not inherently *cause* it, just like nothing exterior actually *causes* stress or happiness. What brings peace or prestige to you might not do it for me

The fact is, feeling the Six Ps is entirely *our* choice, and with the power of choice comes the challenge to progress. It is in the ways we go about meeting this progress challenge that we establish an action's meaning, and even the meaning of our life.

Each of us makes decisions as to what to wear, whom to connect with, what to invest our time in, whom to help, and whom not to help based on whether we believe, consciously or subconsciously, that these acts will bring us these *Six Ps of Progress* – short-term or long-term.

At a mostly subconscious level, we are continuously thinking to ourselves: *Does taking this action (buying this product, switching vendors, hiring this person, calling this help line, agreeing to the terms, etc.) help me move toward pleasure, peace of mind, profit, prestige, and power, or help me to avoid pain?*

And in so doing, we are basically asking ourselves: ***Will taking this action lead to Progress, or will it merely lead to more change?***

The word *PROGRESS* carries a forward thrust and focus, a vibrant and transcendent quality that the words *change* and even *success* don't deliver.

With every *success* comes the desire for more success. When we reach a goal, our natural ambitiousness tells us that the goal is also the stepping stone to the next, possibly more rewarding and worthwhile, goal. Therefore, every success establishes a *new norm,* and brings with it the question: *What next*?

The people we desire to influence and inspire to action (lead, do business with, etc.) must believe that our ideas, our products, our services, our leadership, and our initiatives will help them to move forward. Solid trust must be in place before we can even hope others will choose to alter their lives to include us.

We must be seen as catalysts in others' progress, agents in their progress.
We must be *Progress Agents.*

There is a powerful and important connection between making connections, influential sales and service and solid leadership, personal motivation, and customer loyalty. All are achieved by effectively positioning ideas, recommendations, solutions, products, services – ***even ourselves*** – as progress in the minds of those we wish to inspire to action.

How do we position ourselves, our ideas, our products and services as progress, and not simply as change, in the minds of those we wish to inspire to action?

Pleasure, Peace of Mind, Profit, Prestige, Pain Avoidance and Power...

What about Pride and Purpose? I considered whether I should add Pride and, to a lesser degree, Purpose to the Ps of Progress, and decided not to.

Over the years, I have asked many clients, friends and peers to describe *feeling pride,* and each has described a special combination of pleasure, peace of mind, and prestige –sometimes with a little pain avoidance, profit, and power thrown into the mix.

Pride may be *a solid and realistic sense of one's dignity, value, and self-respect*, but ***the word pride is also associated with feeling lofty, or making an arrogant assumption of superiority.***
Pride often has negative connotations, such as haughtiness, vanity, conceit, egoism, grandiosity, narcissism, being a braggart, and so on.

"Pride is pleasure arising from a man's thinking too highly of himself."
-- Baruch Spinoza

Excessive pride, according to the writings of Aristotle, is commonly the defining trait that leads to a hero's tragic downfall. Heck, pride is one of the Seven Deadly Sins! Pride is even commonly considered the original and most serious of the deadly sins – the source from which all others arise. In the story of Lucifer, pride was what caused his fall from heaven, and his transformation into Satan. This story alone shows *Pride* can be a real downer.

So, given its unhappy history, I felt it best that *Pride* not be included as one of the *Ps of Progress.*

At the same time, *the rightful feeling of pride* – as in self-respect, or pride in one's work or the work of the team – is vital for progress. **When people have little or no self-respect or pride in themselves or their work, they feel increasingly discouraged, powerless, and inferior.**

So pride is tricky. Speaking of the inflated and distorted kind of pride, nineteenth-century author John Ruskin observed: ***"In general, pride is at the bottom of all great mistakes."*** A Hebrew proverb further admonishes: ***"Pride goes before a fall"***

When is pride a negative for you?

The term **Purpose** generally holds different meanings for different people, ***but purpose is not a feeling.***

Purpose is the idea, the objective, the passion behind our actions. Our life's purpose is the core compelling force that pulls us forward.

Purpose is direction *with meaning*. We develop our meaning based upon what we believe will result in us feeling the *Six Ps of Progress*.

Having a Strong, True Sense of Purpose leads to authentically feeling the Six Ps of Progress.

How do you feel when you know, and are following - your purpose?

Progress Agents work to positively influence thoughts and feelings as well as oversee actions. We live in a world of influence. We are influenced to purchase this, to believe that, to participate in this activity, to attend that event. This is not a bad thing. Most often it is good. Our parents influenced our decision not to play with fire. Our best friend influenced our decision not to wear corduroy.

Ever turned a friend on to a restaurant?
You influenced your friend.

Ever go to a movie because a friend said it was good?
That friend influenced you.

> **"There is only one way...to get anybody to do anything. And that is by making the other person want to do it."**
> *-- Dale Carnegie*

Dale Carnegie wrote his classic *How to Win Friends and Influence People* way back in 1936, and its wisdom is no less true and vibrantly powerful today.

The book is packed with insight on leading and building strong relationships by lifting people up, making them feel good, and "spurring people on to success."

The book is not called *How to Lift People Up and Make Them Feel Good* or *How to Spur People on to Success.* No, Carnegie's classic is appropriately titled: *How to Win Friends and Influence People. And who is doing the winning?* It's you and me, along with the person being lifted up, made to feel good, and spurred on to success (*read: influenced*).

In his book, Mr. Carnegie encourages us to, among other things: *Talk in terms of the other person's interests, respect others' opinions, try honestly to see things from the other person's point of view, and try to make the other person happy about doing the things you suggest.* In other words, **genuinely care about people and their feelings.**

But Mr. Carnegie's classic does not only encourage us to take these actions for the benefit of the people we are respecting and *"making happy."* The book doesn't even make the argument that it is even morally right to care about people's feelings *(although I am sure Mr. Carnegie would agree that it is).*

No, the book simply makes the clear case that **caring about others' feelings is good** for the person **winning** friends and **influencing** people.

<u>**Progress Agents**</u> practice a ***"Live and Help Progress"*** philosophy. We thrive on being able to take a challenging situation and proactively work to create outcomes that are positive for all involved (including ourselves). We consistently say and do the things that we believe will help our contacts, companies, clients and coworkers, to grow, advance, make headway, become better, make strides, and progress. We take risks.

"You can never leave footprints that last if you are always walking on tiptoe."
-- *Leymah Gbowee*

Progress Agents know that *To Sell is to Serve.* Success in sales and service is directly tied to influence, connection and attraction. We are attracted to, connected to, and influenced by products, services, ideas, and people that we trust can help us progress.

The great Dottie Walters, one of the legendary founders of the National Speakers Association, shared with me many years ago that the word Sales comes from the Scandinavian root word meaning To Serve.

Soak that in… ***To Serve.***

If we just made that little shift in our own thinking about that word *Sales*, think of how many more people we could serve with our products, services, ideas, and influence and connections!

Important Note on Teamwork & Service:

If we want our exterior customer service to be first rate, our internal customer service must be first rate first.

"We treat our people like royalty. If you honor and serve the people who work for you, they will honor and serve you."
-- Mary Kay Ash

Here are two things I know:

1. **To Sell is to Serve.**
2. **To Serve is *to Be Progress.***

The days of the *"Surefire Closing Statement"* and the *"Glad-handing Slick Salesman"* are thankfully long gone. Today it is imperative for sales and service professionals to truly get to know their contacts, customers and prospects and to help contacts, customers and prospects get to know them.

Selling is therefore a state of mind more than a series of steps. It is a dance, a willingness to help, to influence, to build rapport, to connect, to care.

Those of us who make our careers influencing, making connections and selling are, by and large, outgoing, caring, and driven. We want to help others progress. We believe we can make a difference.

EVERYONE has a need, or a step they desire to take. All must trust we can help them meet that need and take that step.

Contacts, customers and prospects need to trust our belief in ourselves, in our companies, and in our products and services.

To build influence and connection focus on service and trust.

In today's fast-paced, much-hyped, hyper-sensitive and over stimulating world of digital marketing, the ability to make face-to-face connections is a proven and powerful lost art that no person in business should attempt to succeed without.

Making connections effectively puts us apart from the 'smile and dial' boiler-room sales types. Think of *"effective business networking"* as using shared interests to create and cultivate mutually influential and beneficial connections. It is the back-scratch boogie.

Business is a Progress-based Impressions Game – ***a Proof-of-Progress Game*** – The Ultimate Game of Trust.

Progress Agents understand that trust is the basis for all positive long-term relationships (even the one we have with ourselves). We know that the key to effective business networking is to have others *trust* that we ARE and will continue to ***Be Progress.***

Progress Agents know that…**Trust is the promise of progress, not a guarantee of progress.** Trust, just like influence and connection, is fragile, but trust is strengthened by continually being progress for others.

Progress Agents learn about contacts, customers, prospects, employees, coworkers, and friends, uncovering their unique parameters for progress.

The more we can get into the shoes, hearts, and heads of the people we wish to inspire to action, the more we can know what progress means to them. We are then able to relate in ways that show how our initiatives, ideas, products, and services are beneficial and valuable to them.

The road to success is always under construction. We are always striving for something. (I will share that the something I am referring to is not a person, place, or thing, but rather a feeling. A mixture of six feelings, to be exact, but we will deal with that soon enough.)

Continual striving can become quite unpleasant and unhealthy if we do not take time to soak in the positive buzz – feelings – from our forward momentum.

When we focus on daily progress, we are able to feel daily satisfaction. With every forward step, we see more clearly, our confidence grows, our position improves, and our options multiply. We progress toward today's goal on the strength of our past progress. Once achieved, today's goal becomes tomorrow's launching pad.

When a new opportunity comes our way, we internalize it, and size it up as Progress or Change. This new opportunity could be starting a new relationship, buying an electronic gadget, working extra hours on a project, getting up to speed on a new product line, working to meet quota, anything.

**All progress is change,
but not all change is progress.**

Let's say I have an upset stomach. *"Man, I've got a stomachache. Ouch! My stomach is killing me. This has got to change."*

Somebody hears me, walks over, and punches me in the nose. *Is that change?* Yeah, it's change. But it's not progress. Well, maybe to the person who punched me, but not to me.

What may seem like progress (good) to one person or group of people may seem like change (bad) to another. Propaganda, book burning, even war and murder are all thought of as "progress" at some point in the minds of the perpetrators (scary).

Because progress is subjective, there is no single factor that clearly determines whether an event represents progress or change. However, we can say that we:

- ***Start businesses*** *to progress, not change*
- ***Hire employees* to progress, not change**
- ***Work on teams*** *to progress, not change*
- ***Make the tough choices and the tough phone calls*** *to progress, not change*
- ***Keep our cool when dealing with belligerent customers*** *to progress, not change*
- ***Cross the road*** *to progress, not change*
- ***Answer the phone* to progress, not change**
- ***Spend our hard-earned money*** *to progress, not change. (<u>We would rather keep our change than change, but will offer our best to progress</u>.)*
- ***Diet and exercise*** *to progress, not change*

People who claim to be 100% "resistant to (any) change" are often choosing to be resistant to the possibility of progress.

As we age we realize that slowing change can be progress. Think of the forty-year-old swimmer who manages to equal her performance from five years before. Maintenance is progress in that it avoids change for the worse.

We do not want life-changing products, services, experiences, ideas, and opportunities. We want life-progressing products, services, experiences, ideas and opportunities.

We should be careful not to mistake mere change for progress. Just because something is new or flashy does not mean it is right or adds meaning to our lives. We do live in a "next big thing" world.

"It is not strange ... to mistake change for progress."
-- Millard Fillmore

To Change Is Human; to Progress, Divine.

Quick shout out to Alex Pope

If he were among us today, eighteenth-century English poet Alexander Pope would likely be one popular guy on social media. It was he who wrote the lofty words, "To err is human; to forgive, divine." Pope is said to be the third most frequently quoted writer in the English language, after Shakespeare and Tennyson.

Alexander may not be on social media or the internet, but I am, and would be happy to get connected with you:

Join our Facebook Group: **The Progress Agents**

YouTube Channel: **DeanLindsay**

Twitter: **@DeanLindsay**

LinkedIn: **@Dean Lindsay**

Instagram: **@DeanoLindsay**

Facebook: **@DeanLindsayProgressAgent**

Email: **Dean@DeanLindsay.com**

Website: **DeanLindsay.com**

The Rise of Progress Leadership

Change Management Is Dead

The business term "*Change Management*" has been around for a good long while. The term relates to *"initiating significant change"* within an organization's processes, products, service and procedures. This change can include anything from altering work culture to embracing diversity to modifying an individual's work tasks to increasing company morale and loyalty to a new line of products. The goal of *"initiating significant change"* is solid, but where is the influence and connection in the word choice?

The problem with the term "Change Management" is that no one really desires to change or plans to change. ***We desire and plan to progress.***

We do not want managers to manage our change. We want leaders to lead our progress.

Let's call *"initiating significant change"* what it truly is (or should be): ***Progress Leadership.***
In a time of continual transformation, committed leaders – Progress Agents –should focus on inspiring the progress, not apologizing for the change. Progress Agents don't just TELL people what to do. **Progress Agents include others in the *progress* as well as the *process.*** It is reasons that shape, nourish, and sustain the thoughts that create the actions necessary to reach desired results.

"If you want to build a ship, don't drum up people together to collect wood and don't assign them tasks and work, but rather teach them to long for the endless immensity of the sea."
-- Antoine de Saint-Exupéry

Companies are most successful at *"initiating significant change"* when the reasons to act connect personally with the individual employees making the alteration in behavior. If the reasons don't connect with the individual, then the *planned progress* will be viewed as merely change and will be resisted or at least not acted on. Team members may still physically clock in but have often mentally checked out.

Intense focus on feelings in a time of transformation is often described as the *"human side of change management."* This always gives me pause. *The "human side" of change—what other side is there?* Some might say the company side. *So then, the company and the humans are on different sides?* That's the problem right there. **You develop a fuzzy point of view when all you focus on is you.**

Companies are formed by people *(humans)* partnering to get their wants and needs met by helping other people *(humans)* get their wants and needs met. Leaders who do not take the individual into account and do not plan for the human side of *Progress* often find themselves scratching their heads about where their plans went wrong.

"Humanize globalization and globalize humanization."
-- Father Anselm Gruen

It takes more than the title of supervisor, manager, or ***"change agent"*** to lead people in the direction of progress. We all want to be in relationships with people, as well as partner with organizations that bring progress to our lives.

Without personal commitment to execute, new organizational plans and initiatives often fail. Execution is assured by establishing clear links between operations, strategy, and team members. Progress leadership means working to understand and communicate how a team member's personal goals can dovetail with the organization's goals and thus create true commitment that gets the team member to act – because he or she wants to, not because they have to. Progress Leadership means striving to help others find meaning in their work.

Effective leaders focus on helping all progress and not on making some comply.

The most effective leaders are Progress Agents NOT *Change Agents.*

Also, just because a company is getting bigger does not mean it is progressing. A serious challenge for companies large and small is to progress, and not just change. **Moving our focus from change management to progress leadership creates a shift in power from wielding power over employees to creating power among employees.** Progress Agents thus create a ***Be Progress*** work culture in which empowered employees are committed to finding what is truly the next step forward.

All leadership begins with self.
Here are some quick *Progress Agent Handbook Action Steps* for Excelling at **Progress Leadership:**

– **Focus on Leading and Inspiring Progress**
(rather than managing or apologizing for change)..
– **Ask Questions that Show Respect and Value.**
– **Surround Yourself w Self-Motivating Experts.**
– **Help Establish Team Member Expectations.**
– **Care and Listen, Care & Listen Some More.**
– **Encourage *Be Progress* Work Cultures.**
– **Internalize, but Do Not Personalize.**
(Work to not take stuff too personally,
even when someone means it personally.)
– **Get a Massage. Get Another Massage.**
– **Craft and Achieve Big PHAT Goals.**
– **Maximize Your Personal Potential.**
– **Be Passionate About Your Team.**
– **Be Passionate About Your Work.**
– **Be Passionate About Your LIFE.**
– **Drink Water. Drink More Water.**
– **Be Patient and Persistent.**
– **Compliment with Reason.**
– **Eat Right. Eat Breakfast.**
– **Accentuate the Progress.**
– **Be Human. Be Humane.**
– **Take a Long Breath In.**
– **Share Your Expertise.**
– **Look and Feel Sharp**
– **Smile with Reason.**
– **Get Enough Sleep.**
– **Walk and Exercise.**
– **Read Good Stuff.**

- Be Progress.

Influence and the Power of Choice

When considering the meaning of power, many words come to mind: *clout, brawn, capacity, ability, might, power, muscle, steam, horsepower, leadership.* But the word that sums up the true feeling of power, the feeling of influence is the word ***Choice***, the power to determine our own thoughts and actions.

Who has the power of choice? Everyone, we each hold the power of decision making. **Self-discipline is controlling our power of choice.**

"A human being is a deciding being."
-- Dr. Viktor Frankl

Power is not just enforcement. **In the form of influence and persuasion, power is used in countless ways to encourage people to choose to act, feel, and behave in ways other than how they may have initially planned, or would habitually react.** Each of us would make different choices if we were influenced differently. In essence, all human interaction involves power, because ideas hold power, and ideas underlie all language and action.

There is power in branding. There is power in marketing, in PR, in advertising. There is power in "word of mouth" and in social influence. There is power in shared beliefs. Expertise offers power.
Training leads to power. Degrees can translate as power. Positions can hold power.

Power is exercised when we are able to reward and promote. Wealth can bring power. Some feel power from being accepted. Education offers the promise of power because it builds the mental qualities and knowledge to make choices that get things done.

But it is not only knowledge that offers power; being able to communicate knowledge is also power. It is not just what we know or whom we know; it is mainly what we decide to DO with what we know that is paramount.

Power is the ability (present or anticipated) to make choices that bring about significant *change*, usually in people's lives, through one's own actions or those of others.

***Nengli*, the Mandarin word for power, literally means "can-strength," or "being capable."**

To influence others, one must have some understanding and mastery of the situations or things the other person desires or needs.

A boss, manager, or employer wields power over employees because he or she commonly controls projects, working conditions, wages, hiring and firing, etc. However, employees hold power, too. They can quit, slack off, form a union, steal pens and toilet paper, undermine coworkers' morale, provide lousy service, and be all-out liabilities. Employees can also arrive on time, be supportive team players, think outside of the box, and provide world-class service. It all comes down to the power of choice and how that power of choice is influenced.

"Everything can be taken from a man but one thing: the last of the human freedoms – to choose one's attitude in any given set of circumstances, to choose one's own way."
-- Dr. Viktor Frankl

All parties in all relationships have some power. Customers have power to choose to spend their money wherever they please. Companies have the power to alter policies or refuse service.
Power can be delegated, but only to those who choose to accept the power.

One primitive but common way of obtaining the feeling of power is by threatening someone with pain *(firing, a bonk on the head, no dessert).*
There is power in threatening pain.
But this kind of thought and behavior is a negative misuse of power and is always counterproductive. As any student of world history or "office politics" will tell you, such "power" inevitably builds resentment and resistance. And, there is power in resistance.
"Fight the Power" is itself a statement of power.

Someone's awareness of us and our abilities can have powerful results. People carry archives of knowledge and impressions within their gray matter, and it behooves us to have ourselves archived as a source of power.

Powerful people are those with great influence and an easy access to resources, those who can reliably exercise their will, their ideas, and their way.

Progress Agents are able to show how the choices we want others to make will bring them more choices, more power, more progress. But it is still each individual's choice as to what to think and believe, and how to act.

> **"Between stimulus and response there is a space. In that space is our power to choose our response. In our response lies our growth and our freedom."**
> -- *Dr. Viktor Frankl*

Viktor Frankl, M.D., Ph.D. (1905-1997), was an Austrian neurologist, a Holocaust survivor, and one of the greatest European psychiatrists of the twentieth century. The U.S. Library of Congress named Dr. Frankl's enlightening masterpiece, *Man's Search for Meaning,* one of the 10 books that "made the most difference in people's lives."

Dr. Frankl is the founder of logotherapy, which he derived from the words: *logos* – Greek for *reason* or *meaning*, and *therapy* – Greek, meaning *I heal.* Logotherapy therefore means *"Reasons I heal" or "Healing the Meaning*" (trippy, profound, and enlightening both ways).

The basic philosophy of logotherapy is that people have a will to find meaning and that life can have meaning under all circumstances, even the most miserable. Each of us has the freedom, under all circumstances, to choose to find reasons to endure and progress.

"Ever more people today have the means to live, but no meaning to live for."
-- Dr. Viktor Frankl

We have freedom to find meaning in what we do and experience. We have freedom to take a stand when faced with an unjust and possibly unchangeable situation. We each have the power of choice to find our unique meaning in life. Frankl believed we all have more of a desire to *feel powerful* than to *obtain power* (and there is a big difference).

Frankl first used the term logotherapy in 1926, and had developed some of its basic tenets before he was sent to a Nazi concentration camp in 1942. He even had a manuscript devoted to his views sewn into the clothes he wore when he was sent there. However, the Nazis found the manuscript, so Frankl's life's work went up in flames.

Frankl knew he had valuable ideas, but no way of actually sharing them with the world. Early on in his time in the camps he decided to recreate the manuscript, and did so on scraps of paper hidden from guards. He also used the harsh camp environment as his field study.

Frankl worked passionately to prevent inmate suicide and alleviate gloom and depression in fellow prisoners. The Nazis did not allow anyone to actively intervene in an actual suicide attempt, so Frankl's efforts were preventative and kept secret.

He found that very few of his fellow inmates said, *"I want to die."* Most said that they wanted to live, but the ones who eventually survived the camps were those who had focused reasons attached to their survival wish – loved ones to reunite with, something to work for or to look forward to. Frankl theorized that when we have enough meaning attached to an outcome, we are able to withstand the suffering related to achieving it.

Frankl's meaning, his *strong reasons* for surviving, were connected not only to his hope of reuniting with his young wife Tilly, as well as his mother, father and brother, but also to his work. He wanted to survive, had to survive, partly because he had powerful and helpful beliefs about the human condition that he needed to recreate and share with the world.

Freed after three years at Auschwitz, Dachau, and other concentration camps, he returned to Vienna and began work on a book with the literal English translation: *From Death Camp to Existentialism: A Psychiatrist's Experiences in the Concentration Camp.* (In the U.S, we call it *Man's Search for Meaning*.) In the book, Frankl describes *(from the unique perspective of a psychiatrist)* the horrific life of a concentration camp inmate.

With this desire to feel autonomous and powerful, and to work and win in a world of change, we can benefit greatly from a look into Dr. Frankl's teachings.

Three Progress Action Steps from the Work of Dr. Viktor Frankl

1. Harness the Freedom of Choice.
As markets continue to fluctuate, business challenges mount, and personal issues multiply, we each have the freedom to choose our reaction. A resourceful attitude toward a challenge is essential if the challenge is to be met. Dr. Frankl's pregnant wife, his parents and brother were all killed during their incarceration in Nazi prison camps. He'd lost everything, he said, that could be taken from a person, except one thing: *"the last of the human freedoms, to choose one's attitude in any given set of circumstances, to choose one's own way."* We each have the power to choose, but that power is wasted if we do not exercise it.

In the face of inescapable uncertainty (i.e., business challenges, a slowing economy, stiff competition), we must fire up the unwavering determination that comes from possessing strong reasons to overcome our daily challenges. Frankl was a man of action. He believed we must act, must do, must persist.

2. Take Responsibility for Actions.
Frankl taught that life has an urgency to which people must respond if decisions are to be meaningful. Each of us must take responsibility for where we are in our financial situation, in our relationships, and in our career, because it is our decisions that put us there. We have the power of choice and are responsible for those choices. We have not only a right, but a responsibility, to fulfill our individual potential, according to Frankl.

"Life ultimately means taking the responsibility to find the right answers to its problems and to fulfill the tasks which it constantly sets for each individual."

-- Viktor Frankl

Frankl discovered that it is not what happens to us that matters. It is how we respond to what happens that is significant. Same with business. We cannot control all the elements of our personal life or business.

- Trucks break down.
- Water heaters burst.
- Computers crash (so do entire economies).
- Customers move.
- Kids get sick.
- Venders go out of business.
- Things happen.

<u>The only things we can control are our responses, our decisions, our actions. Our actions are our responsibility.</u>

3. Drive Actions by Understanding Goals and Strengths.

Gaining insight into a person's reasons *(especially our own)* goes a long way in helping them progress and reach their full potential. Frankl believed in endurance, but not just for the sake of survival. He believed that all life is shot through with significance, and that this inherent meaningfulness should motivate humans to live and discover that meaning. Frankl warned that some may mistake the surface rewards of materialism, affluence, or hedonism as the true purpose of life.

Those who have suffered loss due to injustice (racial profiling, crime), circumstance (accidents, economy, acts of nature), or the inhumanity of fellow humans know that the search for meaning is not stopped by setbacks. In many cases, as in Frankl's, challenges and adversities serve to inspire and redirect a more determined search for meaning.

> **"Life can be pulled by goals just as surely as it can be pushed by drives."**
> *-- Viktor Frankl*

Great leaders understand the necessity of discovering what their followers are made of, what they're "all about." Frankl firmly believed in the great potential of his fellow humans, and stressed the ability to use one's inner resources to achieve personal goals and find personal truth.

This principle applies equally to every organization. Each member, no matter the responsibility or position, has unique strengths that can prove vital in fueling the progress of the organization.

What drives the people you hope to inspire to action?

What drives you?

A few more Frankl Facts:

During his youth, he wrote to Sigmund Freud. After Freud replied, a lively correspondence developed. Viktor traveled extensively, enjoyed a lifelong passion for mountain climbing, and even obtained his pilot's license while in his sixties.

Dr. Frankl wrote over 30 books. However, in his autobiography, Frankl writes,

"In my view, I was never a big thinker. But one thing I may have been through my life: a thorough and persistent "thinker-through."

(A thinker-through…I like that.)

Viktor Frankl died of cardiac arrest on the 2nd of September, 1997, in Vienna, Austria, at the age of 92.

Viktor Frankl was a Progress Agent!!!

Celebrating Service Excellence

Rock the Customer Experience

Progress Agents know that influence and connection are mission critical in the challenging world of customer service. Customers need the peace and confidence that only our focused attention can provide. Continually showing them that we care, are knowledgeable, and are committed to their progress is the vital force that keeps our relationships and businesses alive. And I know what I'm talking about. I do not wish to brag, but I am a customer. I have been since I got my first allowance, *a couple of you may be customers too.*

As customers, we want the peace of mind that comes from a customer-service representative listening to our issues and championing our cause. We want the peace of mind that comes from believing that a sales representative is acting in our best interest. We want the peace of mind that comes from employees looking and acting like they want to be there, and who are passionate about their work.

But let's not think for a minute that providing solid customer service is something done *only* for the customer. We shouldn't kid ourselves. Providing solid customer care adds to our influence and peace of mind, too. Many of our goals are achieved by serving customers. **We reach our full potential when service becomes habitual.**

One of the major reasons we even wear the *"Serve others"* hat is so that later in the day we can wear the *"Serve me"* hat. Our service to others, serves us.

It helps to keep the personal benefits of providing unparalleled service front and center in our minds. There are times we do not feel like serving customers, but we always want to serve ourselves. There are even times when the customer (who may be surly, rude, drunk) does not deserve our best. But we always desire the best for ourselves. Therefore, it can be helpful to remind ourselves of the role that earning and maintaining customer loyalty plays in our personal peace of mind and progress.

Want to get closer to job security? **Serve customers**.
Want less stress? **Rock the Customer Experience.**
Want your 401(K) to grow? **Earn customer's loyalty.**
Worried about downsizing? **Provide Customers Care.**
Want your company to be more profitable? **Ditto.**
How about bonuses or better tips? **Same.**
Want to have more fun at work? **Serve those bosses, I mean customers, I mean bosses.**
Want more money for advertising? **Serve.**
Want to diminish the need for advertising? **Serve.**
Want your customers to feel peace of mind? **Serve.**
Want job satisfaction?
You guessed it... Serve Those Customers!

Offering customers the promise of peace of mind, offers us peace of mind. That is why we strive for customer loyalty, so that we KNOW we have a customer base that is solid, jazzed, and growing. That knowledge sure helps me sleep well at night. *How about you?*

Know this... **If we treated all our customers as if they were our best customers, we would have a lot more best customers!!**

Customers are Revenue, Referrals and Reality. When we lose sight of the personal benefits of providing quality service, we begin to disregard the concerns of our customers. Unfortunately for everyone, this makes customers unhappy, leads to legitimate complaints and ultimately losing the customer.

Just saying we provide good customer service doesn't cut it anymore. Every company, every organization says they provide good customer service, or *great* customer service, or even *stellar* customer service.

You never hear of a company touting their lame service. *"Our customer service generally sucks. But we do have our good days, so how's about buying something?"*

Many adjectives have been plopped in front of the words "customer service" to help rally some form of interest in providing positive service to customers. They include: ***Astonishing, Superior, Exceptional, Positively Outrageous, Super, Multicultural, World-Class, Magnetic, Effective, Branded, Practical, Nonpareil, Breakthrough, Remarkable, Magical, Quality, Effective, Five-Star, and Not So Cruddy.*** (OK. I made up that last one, but you just wait. Someone will snag it. Next year you'll see an ad for a hot new business book: *How to Be Not So Cruddy: 7 Habits of Barely Tolerable Professionals.*)

Progress in service leads to progress in sales.

A thorough definition of *customer service* is full of intangibles, and it is those intangibles that make or break a business. In today's competitive marketplace, *service* is the most important thing a company has to *offer*.

Many companies win customers with special offers, only to lose that new business to their competitor by providing lousy service. Quality customer service makes the all-important difference when two, ten, or twenty businesses seem to offer the same product or professional service.

The need is undeniable, the concepts are easy to understand, and the training sound, but still, proactive customer service is just not happening. All expect good service but few are willing to give it. It helps to widen our perspective as to what a customer is.

Anyone affected, positively or negatively, by the work we do (including our families and ourselves) can be thought of as our "customer."

Within this wider perspective, we see that real service is based on integrity, care, and sincerity, none of which can be measured with money. Nor can it be automated, no matter how soft-spoken and attractive the audio-animatronic voice may be.

Unfortunately, it seems that when an organization labels some of its professionals as *customer-service reps* or *customer advocates,* the rest of the organization assumes they are let off of the "customer care" hook. Not true.

We are ALL in the customer-service business. There is no other business. In fact, there is NO business without the customer.

Every member of our organization is a "customer-service representative," no matter what their title or job description may be.

We are all working for the man (or woman), and that person's name is **customer** *(or client, or guest, or partner, or stockholder, or employee, or team member).*

> **"There is only one boss – the customer. And he can fire everybody in the company – from the chairman on down – simply by spending his money somewhere else."**
> -- *Sam Walton*

Customers are NOT dependent on us; WE are dependent on THEM!!!

Progress Agents *know the* ***Best Marketing*** *is a* ***Rocking Customer Experience!!*** An attitude of service is not one of servitude but an attitude of goodwill and a willingness to help others progress.

As a service to whomever is interested in co-writing:
How to be *Not So Cruddy:*
7 Habits of Barely Tolerable Professionals,
with me, here is an outline of the 7 Habits.

Habit 1:
Be Slow to React to Customer Concerns.

Habit 2:
Begin with the End of the Business Day in Mind.

Habit 3:
Put First Things Last and Don't Get Around.
to Them

Habit 4:
Think Lose/Win or Win/Lose –
Somebody Has Got to Lose!

Habit 5:
Seek First to Tell. Then Hang Up.

Habit 6:
Scrutinize Customer Needs to See If They Warrant Effort.

Habit 7:
Sharpen the Tongue to Use on Customers and Coworkers.

Time to Progress

Progress Agents know that time is the great equalizer. Each day, every one of us gets the same amount – 24 hours – 1440 minutes. Nobody gets less. Nobody gets more. Time can not be slowed, stopped, sped up, or saved like money. Time's ticking, always ticking.

What is an effective use of your time?
The answer is totally subjective because the value of the results is subjective. What makes a wise investment of time for me may not be a wise investment for you. Each of us is, however, investing some of our time in daily activities that do not serve our goals of growing in influence and connections.

All of us have said to ourselves, *"Oh, I know I need to get connected to more people, if I could only FIND the time."* Time does not need to be *found*. It is right here.

Time, we don't find it or make it, we schedule it and take it!!

Time needs to be invested wisely. Each day we are *choosing* to invest our time somewhere, and for a reason.

By managing our time more wisely, we minimize stress, improve our quality of life, and have time to *progress*. Unfortunately, time management is one of those life skills that no one teaches us in school.

Time Management is really Self-Management, with a respect for time.

Four Progress Agent Handbook Time to Progress Tips:

1. "To Do" or Not "To Do"

In the late 1920s, Charles Schwab, president of the then fledgling Bethlehem Steel Company (unrelated to the discount brokerage of the same name), asked management consultant and efficiency expert Ivy Lee to help him and his team become more productive.

After observing Schwab for several hours, Ivy told him that he could teach a time-management system in about 20 minutes that would enable Schwab and his executives to get 50% more work done, without working harder or longer. Schwab asked what this advice would cost him. Lee replied, *"Use the plan for six months and send me a check for how much you think it is worth."*

Lee recommended the following:

1. Write down the things you have to do the following day.
2. Number these tasks in the order of their real importance.
3. Start your day by working on the first item on your list and stick with it until it's accomplished (or until you've done as much as you can); then go on to the next one, and so on.

Six months later, Lee received a check from Schwab for $25,000, equivalent to $500,000 in today's world.

A half a million dollars – for a To-Do List tip?
I should have charged more for this book!

Charles Schwab and his executives took Ivy's "To-Do List" advice, and within five years turned Bethlehem Steel Company into the biggest steel producer in the world.

A To-Do List is common sense, right?
But is it common practice?

The key is to address the most important thing first, and not to look over the additional fifteen "To-Do" items until Number One is completed. That way, we won't see Number Twelve and say, "*Oh, that won't take very long, so I'll do that first. It's easier.*"

Prioritizing ensures that we are investing our time and energy in those tasks and steps that bring the biggest benefits to our lives. *If we don't know what we should be doing, how can we manage our time to do it?*

"If you want to make good use of your time, you've got to know what's most important and then give it all you've got."
-- Lee Iacocca

It is OK, and normal, to have stuff left on your list at the end of the day. If you follow Ivy's system, you have worked on the most important thing already. The other stuff flows through to the next day. Figure out what works for you and don't "make a big to-do" (old idiom for "complain too much") about it. Just do the "To Do."

2. Focus on Being Effective More Than Being Efficient. There's a big difference between "effectiveness" and "efficiency." When we are efficient, we are able to carry out tasks in a short time. However, we won't be effective unless those actions result in us moving closer to our goals.

Efficiency basically means producing outcomes quickly.

Effectiveness basically means producing desired outcomes.

Sometimes, becoming more efficient leads to becoming less effective. For example, in this fast pace of life and business, we naturally seek more efficient ways to communicate. We send e-mails rather than make phone calls, and have Skype meetings rather than meeting face-to-face.

Although these may appear to be more efficient ways to communicate, they may actually be less effective than the methods they replace.

Clearly, being both effective and efficient should be the aim, but if effectiveness is lost for the sake of efficiency, then the whole purpose for doing whatever it is we're doing is defeated.

Sales calls can be made very efficiently, twenty-five an hour. But if sales or appointments are the goal, the calls are not very effective. We can deal with customer issues efficiently, but not necessarily effectively.

Sometimes we are simply doing the wrong things. In his book, *The 4-Hour Workweek,* Timothy Ferriss shares how we shouldn't waste time being efficient in tasks that are not effective, and that we should work to limit or eliminate such time-wasters.

The 80-20 Rule, or Pareto Principle, states that 80 percent of the reward or effect from any endeavor comes from 20 percent of the effort. The trick to being effective is to isolate and identify that valuable 20 percent and put most of your energy into <u>those</u> efforts. There is definitely a need for efficiency. But efficiency is never the goal. Effectiveness is what is ultimately important, and effectiveness is personal. Nothing vital should be given up for the sake of being efficient. ***Better to do the right thing wrong, than the wrong thing right.*** Of course, it is best to do the right things right. **Gain influence by mastering ways to efficiently be more effective at "being progress."**

<u>80+20 words on the Pareto Principle</u>

Twentieth-century management consultant Joseph M. Juran coined this well-established principle, naming it after Italian economist and philosopher Vilfredo Pareto. Pareto had observed that 80% of his country's wealth was controlled by 20% of its population. Juran, whose teachings focused on managing for quality, expanded Pareto's principle, applying it to productivity issues. (For example, 80% of our sales come from 20% of our customers.) Although the principle is also known as "the vital few and the trivial many," Joseph Juran preferred "the vital few and the useful many" as a way to show that the remaining 80% should not be ignored.

3. Make a Molehill Out of the Mountain.

JOKE - *Q: How do you eat an elephant?*
A: One bite at a time.

Most of the time, starting projects is more challenging than finishing them. We see this big project we'd love to accomplish, we doubt we will ever finish it, so we don't even start. The key to *putting off putting off* is to break projects into manageable chunks, so we are not overwhelmed by them. Start!

"He who has begun has half done. Dare to be wise; begin!"
-- Horace

4. Dare to Take Time. If we don't have the time to do it right, we don't have time to do it wrong. Doing our work right the first time often takes more time upfront, but correcting a flurry of careless errors usually results in more time spent in the long run. I know it may sound odd, but often good time management means responding slower to some tasks.

For example, if we are investing time in a high-priority activity, we might not answer the phone while we're doing it. We need to take the time we need to do a quality job.

"Until we manage time, we can manage nothing else."
-- Peter Drucker

Influence is DISCy Business

We each have our own style, our own way we like to communicate with others, our own way of being influenced as well as influential *(different strokes for different folks).* This is a basic human fact.

It is also a fact that we need to make a positive impression when we meet someone. Unfortunately, a tremendous amount of human energy is used unproductively in talking past or "at" each other. We often fail to make a real connection with someone because we have a set of behavioral preferences that do not mesh with those of the person on the other side of our bifocals. ***No Connection = No Influence.***

Progress Agents utilize a keen awareness of individual behavioral differences and, without being chameleons, modify their own preferences to make a favorable impression. Even though we are all unique, most people do fit into a certain style or predictable pattern of behavior. People with similar styles tend to exhibit specific types of behavior common to that style. Such patterns of behavior influence how people prefer to communicate and interact.

We need to strive to understand and embrace these different behavioral styles. This makes us better able to interact with other folks, even those who appear to be very different and sometimes hard to understand. When we identify the behavioral differences in ourselves and others, we can adapt our style to create a comfortable environment for the person we are speaking with.

A solid understanding of the DISC behavioral model is useful for aligning with others through solid first impressions. DISC measures observable behavior and emotions. The development of the DISC model is based on the work of American psychologist Dr. William Marston, an expert in behavioral styles.

In 1926, Marston published *The Emotions of Normal People,* in which he grouped people along two axes: either active or passive tendencies relative to their favorable or unfavorable view of the environment.

Say what? Here is a view of DISC from 30,000 feet:

Some people are *Reserved* and some are *Outgoing*.
One type is not better than the other.
Some people are *People-Oriented* and some are *Task-Oriented*.
One type is not better than the other.

Each of us is a unique blend of*:*
Reserved or Outgoing, mixed with the quality of being People-Focused or Task-Focused.

Marston's DISC research showed how behavioral characteristics may be grouped into four fundamental styles (D.I.S.C.):

- **Dominance**
- **Influence**
- **Steadiness**
- **Conscientiousness**

D - Dominance

These are the Task-Oriented, Outgoing Types.

These folks are direct, demanding, determined, and decisive. They are confident, competitive, take-action doers. They will likely ask WHAT questions more than HOW questions.

Some famous DOMINANT Behavior types are:
Kevin O'Leary, Barbara Corcoran, Mark Cuban (heck the whole Shark Tank), Vince Lombardi, Henry Ford

To deliver a solid first impression to D-types:
Be concise and direct. These people need prestige, authority, and control.

I - Influence

These are the People-Oriented, Outgoing Types.

These folks are interactive, inspirational, impressive, and interested in people. They are friendly, outgoing, emotional "talkers."

Some famous INFLUENTIAL Behavior types are:
Oprah Winfrey, Will Farrell, Sally Field (You like me. You really like me!), Dean Lindsay, Wayne Brady.

To deliver a solid first impression to I-types:
Skip the details, socialize, and show excitement. These people need recognition, acceptance, and to be heard.

S - Steadiness

These are the Reserved, People-Oriented Types. These folks are stable, sensitive, and supportive. They are loyal, dependable, and good listeners.

Some famous STEADY Behavior types are: *Mister Rogers, Mother Teresa, Joan of Arc, Albert Schweitzer, Florence Nightingale, Mahatma Gandhi*

To deliver a solid first impression to S-types: Be reassuring and take it slow. These people need security, appreciation, and time to decide if there should be a relationship.

C - Conscientiousness

These are the Reserved, Task-Oriented Types. These folks are competent, careful, calculating, contemplative, and cautious. They are analytical, detailed, and do not show emotions readily. They are likely to ask HOW questions more than WHAT questions.

Some famous CONSCIENTIOUS Behavior types are: *Columbo (OK, not a real dude, but you get the point), Tom Landry, Isaac Newton, Johann Sebastian Bach, Michelangelo, Sherlock Holmes (again, not a real guy).*

To deliver a solid first impression to C-types: Be prepared and structured. These people need facts and are committed to quality.

Of course, all typologies are approximations. People vary along these four dimensions rather than fitting wholly into one. However, understanding the four different behavioral styles makes us better able to make positive impressions, even with those who we see as "different" or hard to understand.

Being sensitive to these differences creates a relaxed environment where people want to move the relationship forward and offer their best.

Recognize and respect individual nuances, make adjustments, use good judgment, and adapt. Learning and incorporating the DISC model of behavior is valuable for increasing trust and keeping communication open.

In my work over the years within organizations, I have had the opportunity to research DISC extensively and train on the DISC model in several of my customized customer service, sales and workplace culture development programs. Please contact me for further information on DISC training.

A few interesting side notes:
Much later in his life, Dr. Marston created "Wonder Woman" while serving as an educational consultant for DC Comics. Authoring the Wonder Woman comic, Marston used a pen name: Charles Moulton.

"Most of us actually stifle enough good impulses during the course of a day to change the current of our lives."
-- *Dr. William Marston*

The desire to understand the reasons for our diverse behavior has been an age-old preoccupation.

The explanations of the ancients were interesting:

Empedocles (444 B.C.), the founder of a school of medicine in Sicily, believed that everything is made of earth, air, fire, and water. These external elements combine in an infinite number of ways, thus explaining the diversity of behavior.

In 400 B.C. the Greek physician Hippocrates concluded that it is not external factors that shape behavior.

He disagreed with many of his day who believed human behavior was determined by being born under a certain astrological configuration of planets. Hippocrates theorized that it was something that takes place "inside" the individual.

Hippocrates believed that if people had a fast, hot fluid running inside their body, they would be direct, decisive, and a leadership-type person. If one had a fluid that was warm and slow, that person would be family- and relationship-oriented.

Even though Hippocrates' 'blood theory' didn't hold much water, it was the first substantial method for identifying and grouping types of human behavior.

Presence Power

How we hold our physical body communicates a tremendous amount of information about us. Be aware of presence power. Studies suggest that a person will unconsciously interpret approximately 55% of the meaning of your message from physiological cues from your attire, body position, weight, stance, and facial expressions.

Body language, demeanor, and dress are important elements in making a lasting progress-based impression. First impressions are often lasting impressions. So, take pride in your appearance. Be fun and sociable.

You are the number-one element in your success strategy.

How you look and present yourself matters. You want to look smart and with-it. You should not look untidy. No messed-up hair, wrinkled shirts, or loose ties. I believe the most ideal and influential wardrobe choice for effective business networking is slightly better dressed than the other attendees.

Check yourself before you go out. Do a 360 in front of a full-length mirror. *Would you want to talk to you? Would you want to be seen talking to you?*

"Charm them with your presence as soon as they look at you."
- Anna Held

Ask someone's opinion. Take the advice of others about your appearance. *I ask my wife. She has saved me from more than a few bad shirt/jacket combos.*

However, do not rely on your "together" look to cover up for sad puppy behavior or poor conversational ability.

Stand, speak, and act as if you were self-confident, attractive, vital. If you have *flair*, use it. Make sure you will be remembered in a positive way.

Be enthusiastic. An enthusiastic attitude distinguishes the really *effective* networkers from the *so-so* networkers.

> **"The key is to keep company only with people who uplift you, whose presence calls forth your best."**
> -- ***Epictetus***

Speak with a positive countenance, exhibit confidence, and display a natural enthusiasm about your life and your work. Be a walking-talking representation of life, in all its excitement and possibility.

How you say something means as much or more than what you say. **You are your best public relations representative.** You are the person who knows best what you do and what you have to offer others.

Finding the Funny Shows Presence Power.
Humor attracts and holds attention. Many a person has walked away from a conversation out of sheer boredom. Making someone laugh *(with you, not at you)* is progress. Make them laugh and they will like you. Humor can help make a great impression because it appeals to a person's need for pleasure and release.

Think I am just joking around? Humor has been scientifically proven to relieve stress, motivate, and improve relationships. The use of good humor relaxes people; in that state, they become more open. A tense or uncomfortable person is far less able or willing to have a good discussion with you.

"Laughter is the shortest distance between two people."
-- Victor Borge

Common sense is a prerequisite for using humor successfully. Avoid any attempt at political, sexual, or religious humor. Refrain from making off-color or derogatory remarks about others. Trying to get a chuckle at the expense of others shows a lack of professionalism, character, and good sense.

No jokes. Tell stories. A joke is rarely original, memorable, or all that funny. (Of all the jokes you've been told in your life, how many do you remember?) Most jokes don't help the person you are talking to get to know you. Jokes make you look like you are trying too hard. They are contrived.

Jokes force your audience into the uncomfortable position of having to smile or chuckle when they're not amused. They act more as a shield than anything. Jokes are often risky because most are demeaning to some group of people. Stories are where it's at. They are genuine and offer a window into the real you.

The highest form of humor is to laugh at yourself; the lowest form is to laugh at someone else. Tell personal stories where the lesson is learned, or the embarrassment is suffered at your own expense. It will make you appear more vulnerable, more approachable, more human. Poke fun at yourself and people will laugh with you, not at you.

Don't be afraid of putting some egg on your own face early in the conversation. Self-deprecating humor is so effective that it is highly regarded as a leadership trait. It reflects confidence and strength. It shows that you are secure enough to laugh at yourself. It also creates instant rapport, defuses tension, and makes you more likable. Learn to laugh at what you do, without laughing at who you are.

Quick One Liner:

"I'm such a bad speller, my spell checker is stunned."

Tell stories that gently poke fun at yourself. Doing this acts as a social lubricant and shows that you are comfortable in your own skin and at ease with life. It encourages your listener to feel the same way. "Laugh and the world laughs with you."

Rehearse your lines. In meeting people, we each have certain situations that seem to come up again and again. You can anticipate these situations and be ready with witty, fresh, well-rehearsed, "spontaneous" comebacks.

"There are three things that are real – God, human folly, and laughter. The first two are beyond comprehension. So we must do what we can with the third."
-- John F. Kennedy

Humor takes intelligence and subtle qualities like insight and sensitivity. Using humor displays a mastery of language and an openness to the human condition. If someone is "naturally funny," they are probably really intelligent.

Study humor**, be-* as the poet Robert Frost wrote, "never more serious than when joking."***

Study humor. Appreciate humor. Seek it out.
What was so funny? ***Why did you laugh?***
Why did you not laugh? ***Why did you groan?***

People are often envious of those who are funny and able to make others laugh Humor is a technique that can be learned, developed, and perfected just like origami *(OK, not like origami, but you get the idea).*

We attract more connections and opportunities as we incorporate more joy and humor into our daily lives.

Once we cultivate humor, we have the foundation for intellectual rapport. Not every attempt will get a knee-slapping belly laugh; our mission is bigger than that. A comedian succeeds just by being funny, but a connector succeeds only when the humor helps to create a positive progress-based impression.

But of course, humor will never substitute for solid listening skills. Mix too much yuck-yuck with too little care or respect and you will plummet, crash, and burn.

Some people will not be influenced or enjoy humor. It will not take a rocket scientist to spot these folks because they will be the cats that won't laugh at anything. The best thing to do in this scenario is to play it straight. Cut the humor and ask another open-ended question that gets them talking. Remember, the goal is to deliver a solid progress-based impression.

"Humor is just another defense against the universe."

- Mel Brooks

Our minds can only focus on one thing at a time. When we find the humor in a situation, it automatically relieves stress because the humor takes the place of stress, washing it away in waves of laughter and sometimes even rivers of tears. Laughter is good medicine.

Humor is a learned coping skill that improves with practice. When we laugh, similar to when we exercise, endorphins are released in the brain that help us feel better about the situation and offer more energy to tackle challenges. "Belly laughs" are also said to give our innards a good workout, massaging our organs while warming our hearts. *Touching, isn't it?*

"A person without a sense of humor is like a wagon without springs – jolted by every pebble on the road."
-- *Henry Ward Beecher*

Progress Agents who maintain a sense of humor gain influence and respect. People are drawn to – and build solid relationships with people who are upbeat and have a positive presence and jovial frame of mind.

Find what makes you laugh.
And be sure to laugh at yourself from time to time.

What makes you laugh?

Where is the humor in the situation?

Sit or stand up straight. Gesture with power and confidence. Be fully engaged. Nod in agreement. Smile. Do not fold your arms or let your eyes wander off into the distance; look like you are having a good time. People trust people who look them in the eye.

Do not shift focus. The more you change your focus, the more new information your brain is taking in. If you change focus frequently, you can overload your brain to the point where you are "at sea" and unable to focus on the issue at hand.

Be careful about shifting your weight while chatting with someone. It communicates a lack of interest and confidence, and it can result in your contact feeling a lack of TRUST.

Also, do not keep your hands in your pockets the whole time and jingle-jangle-jingle your keys or change. *You are not there to provide musical backup or percussion for the event.*

Think about this:
Each positive first impression has the potential to turn into a priceless business relationship. People want to do business with professionals who are excited about life and who look like they have their act together.

"We never know which lives we influence, or when, or why."
-- Stephen King

CONNECTION

con·nec·tion

1. a relationship in which a person, thing, or idea is linked or associated with something else.
2. the action of linking one thing with another.
3. people with whom one has social or professional contact or to whom one is related, especially those with influence and able to offer one help.

"Networking has been cited as the number one unwritten rule of success in business. Who you know really impacts what you know."
-- Sallie Krawcheck

"Coming together is a beginning; keeping together is progress; working together is success."
-- Edward Everett Hale

The Long Road from Met to Net

There is this unassuming little word you often find in the biographies of influential people. The word is "met."

Then William R. Hewlett met David Packard.
Then Dean Martin met Jerry Lewis.
Then Sid met Nancy.
Then Barnum met Bailey..
(google them- all worth knowing about)

We meet people all the time. Meeting people is part of life. Making true connections is one of the fundamental steps on the road to success.

So why is meeting new people in a networking situation so intimidating?
Why is it so tough?
How do some people make it look so easy?
What is their secret?

We *meet* people all the time. They are everywhere. Meeting people may be necessary in successful business networking, but it is not the only step.
There is a long road from *Met to Net.*

There is a big difference between meeting someone and making a **true connection** that leads to a priceless professional relationship.

"Succeeding in business is all about making connections."
-- *Richard Branson*

How do you build a powerful business network?

This is an important question to consider because, to a large degree, who you know influences and helps determine who you become in life.

"We think of ourselves as individuals, but we are embedded in networks of relationships that define and sustain us."
-- Michael Nichols

The most influential, well-rounded and happy people are most often the ones who are best connected to other influential, well-rounded and happy people. When these people need support or information, they know the right people to call.

How well-connected you are determines your access to those with the most money, the best contacts, the real power and influence *(not to mention the best seats at sporting events).* Being connected to the right people opens up opportunities for you and your company.

"A noble person attracts noble people and knows how to hold onto them."
-- Johann Wolfgang von Goethe

Building solid relationships with other professionals in your field is also a crucial part of career development and job-hunting. During tough economic times, your network has the power to help you make a positive move and provide a stepping stone to your next career. Best to develop your network before you need it.

If you are already looking for a new job, deep down in your blood pumper you already know that you need to get out there and connect with people.

Sure, in a perfect world, your track record and past successes would speak for themselves, but without professional and personal contacts, your best two-page spiffy resume on off-white professional-grade paper is likely going to just take up space in a pile on a hiring manager's over stimulated desk.

You are going to have to log off Monster, move away from the keyboard, and find a room to work.

For many professionals, effective business networking is something of an enigma because the skills needed to network successfully are simple to understand but not necessarily easy to consistently implement.

Making face-to-face connections is an art as well as a skill. Take the time to develop the art of effective networking.

Making connection is a creative process. You are creating ways to serve and to help people progress. You progress when you help others progress. Each of us has wonderfully unique gifts to share with others.

When we have made someone feel good, helped them progress or solve a problem, they talk about us in a good way to all the people who are in their network. We gain influence and connection.

As William Allman, the author of *Stone Age Present,* states, "***The key to our species' success is our great skill in making close alliances with others.***" *True enough.* There are many valuable benefits to effective business networking:

1. Connection & Influence *(Friendship & Support)*
2. Advice and Access to Fresh and Unique Points of View
3. New Career paths, Employment, and Business Opportunities
4. Referrals and introductions to New Strategic Alliances & Quality Prospects
5. Important Information *(Market/organizational shifts, upcoming events, etc.)*
6. Promotions or Lateral Moves within Your Organization,
7. Unique Sales and Service Ideas from Professionals in Other Fields
8. Introductions to Quality Vendors and Resources
9. Advocates within Related Organizations and Industries
10. More Sales & Better Recruitment!!

"The final frontier may be human relationships, one person to another."
-- Buzz Aldrin

Networking's Bum Rap

For far too long the term "Business Networking" has gotten a bum rap. I have consistently asked sales and service professionals I am coaching or working with to share with me what they think of when they hear the words 'business networking.' Far too often I hear it conjures up images of manipulative, self-serving, insincere and predatory individuals, who are on the prowl for someone they can pounce on, try to sell something to, or solicit an unearned favor from or influence over.

When meeting someone new, ineffective business networkers will rapidly scan new acquaintances to prejudge their usefulness while regurgitating their blanket sales pitch and robotically handing out their business card before abruptly moving on to their next victim. This is a waste of time for the ineffective networker and the unfortunate people they corner.

Here is an actual conversation I had with an ineffective business networker.

Me: *Tell me about the business networking event yesterday.*
Ineffective Networker: *I did great. I handed out 35 cards.*
Me: *Did you strike up some good conversations?*
Ineffective Networker: *What? I was busy. I handed out 35 cards.*
Me: *OK. How many cards did you get?*
Ineffective Networker: *Ah, I think two.*

Progress Agents judge their success not by how many cards they give out, but by how many they have collected and the relationships they have potentially created. After connecting with someone and getting their business card, reconnecting with them is paramount.

Business networking can be a lifelong skill that allows shortcuts to important people and information. Anything is possible through business networking. It should make life easier. The key is to cultivate relationships by sharing ideas, information, and resources. Work to set up "win-win" situations where all parties benefit from the exchange, whether immediately or sometime in the future.

Effective Business Networking *is NOT* forcing yourself or your products on someone.

Effective Business Networking *IS* getting to know people, their lives, and their needs.

Effective Business Networking *is NOT* selling your products and services.

Effective Business Networking *IS* selling yourself.

Effective business networking saves time and money while reducing frustration. Everyone networks. Every professional, in every type of career and in every aspect of commerce, networks. Every occupation has networking opportunities. Dentists, plumbers, and taxidermists all have their annual meeting of some kind where they get together and chew the industry fat.

Before we go any further, answer this question:
Do I genuinely want to understand and help fulfill the needs of others?

If you do – *good.* You have the makings of an influential progress agent as well as an effective business networker.
A nurturing, giving attitude is the cornerstone to going from met to net, contact to connection and becoming an effective business networker.

If you don't – you are going to have a tough time making networking work for you. But there is still hope...Read on!

All effective business networkers help others progress. Gaining influence and connections through effective business networking is not a one-way street. It's more like an eight-lane superhighway speeding in both directions - both people need to benefit.

Progress Agents know effective business networking is positively reciprocal.

When making new acquaintances, many people unwisely focus *only* on their own personal gain. It is far wiser to learn to appreciate the other person and learn what you can do to be supportive. Relationships need nurturing.

Effective business networking requires patience, persistence and progress-based action.

Again, start with a smile. Sounds simple, and it is, very simple. People like people who smile at them. It makes them smile back and smiling is pleasurable. Pleasure is progress. If you smile when you first see someone, it helps them feel good and that is a solid start.

> **"Stick your teeth in the air.**
> **Show the world you care."**
> *-- Eddie Coker*

Give before you receive.
Successful networkers know they must contribute before they can expect a return on their investment. Try to match and connect the knowledge and skills of the various people you meet with others you have already established relationships with.

Give a smile - Get a smile.
Give help - Get help.
Introduce people to people - People introduce people to you.
Care - Get cared for.
Listen - Get listened to.
Help others progress – Progress.
Give referrals - Get referrals.

Ask yourself:
Do people perceive me as a generous helper or more as a selfish taker?

Careful here. If you wear the *selfish taker* label, people will eventually whittle you out of their loop. This is exactly the opposite outcome you are looking for.
Start today. Say it loud. Say it proud.

I am a progress agent. I like to help. Today I am going to help and give – and then help and give some more.

Get out and meet people. Network everywhere! Look people in the eye. Be genuinely interested. Building visibility and credibility builds profitability. Make sure you are making a positive impression.
People need to be aware of you in a positive way.

**People must *be aware* of you,
not *beware* of you.**

The most successful individuals in any industry are those who become progress agents – and stay progress agents.

They maintain their visibility and credibility.
They help people.
They share information.
They show they care.
They consistently do the things that are necessary to demonstrate that they're in the relationship for the long term.

It's not that tough. Most people on the planet get pleasure when people smile at them, listen to them, and take interest in what they say. So that's a pretty safe place to start.

"One of the most beautiful compensations of this life is that no one can sincerely try to help another without helping himself."
-- Ralph Waldo Emerson

Effective business networking is nothing new. Most of our relationships began through networking and referrals. Heck, *Paul McCartney met John Lennon through networking.* Effective business networking is simply two or more parties meeting for mutual influence and benefit. *It is natural to want to share, help, give, and contribute.*

Effective business networking sure beats cold-calling. Wow. Cold-calling over the phone is tough. Most sales professionals find it taxing and most consumers don't like it much either.

Think about it. *Do you like to be cold-called? Does it work on you?*

Cold Caller: *Mr. Jun..dson?*
Mr. Johnson: *That's Johnson.*

Cold Caller: *Oh…(giggle) sorry. Is Mr. Johnson there?*
Mr. Johnson: *No. (Click.)*

Consumers dislike being solicited by phone so much that a law was passed enabling them to get their names on a "Do Not Call" list. A whole bunch of people got themselves on that list as soon as they could. *Maybe even you. I know I did.*

These consumers invested the time to get on this list to say a big, fat ***"NO thank you! Please do not call me."***

A solid and gracious way around the Do Not Call list is to get out and meet people. You can earn a fortune – *and have some fun in the process* – building relationships with quality business professionals through effective business networking.

And don't get me started on ROBOCALLS!!!

***Folks do not like robo-calls in the morning.
They don't like them while they're snoring.
They do not like them while watching TV.
Not even 'courtesy calls' from AT&T.
They do not like them about how to invest,
Or how to save more than all the rest.
They would not like calls with a special rate.
They would not like them with an expiration date.
Not with a special offer,
Not from a hacking cougher.
They do not like this telemarketing Spam.
They do not like it, Spam I am.***

-- Thank you, Dr. Seuss.

There is power in numbers. When you effectively build relationships with others, you have the opportunity to connect with and influence many more people than you could ever connect with or influence on your own. After a while, your networking "web" will naturally interconnect and seem to go on and on, even when you are not actively working it. Influential connections are continuously being made.

Do not underestimate the power of your contact. It is well documented that most people have some form of relationship with around 250 people *(widely referred to as their Circle of Influence).* These are not 250 people they would invite to their Christmas – Hanukkah – or even Festivus party *(just a little something for the Classic Seinfeld fans)*.

These are 250 people they know directly or indirectly, ranging from family members to random contacts that involve some amount of persuasion. This persuasion is used all the time to recommend a good restaurant, shoe store, plastic surgeon, energy drink, personal trainer, CPA, handyman, florist or *(insert your profession here).*

Theoretically, each of your 250-some-odd contacts *could* recommend you and your services to 250 additional people.

That is cool to think about and empowering to consider! ***But here's the rub:*** Just because they COULD recommend you, your products, and your services to 250 others does not mean that they ARE or that they WILL.

Some quick questions to ask yourself:

- *Do people have a TRUSTing impression of me and my services? Why, or why not?*
- *Do they see me, my company, and my services as providing progress?*
- *Do they VALUE what I do for them and others?*
- *Enough to recommend me to others?*
- *Enough to use my service themselves?*
- *Do they VALUE their relationship with me?*
- *Do they feel that a relationship with me means progress for them?*

Influence and connection dance well with trust and value.

How do we build trust?
How do we establish value?
Trust is a feeling. It is a buzz.
Trust is fluid. It is fragile.
Value is established in the mind of the beholder.
Trust between people is built moment by moment, year to year. True value is established over time.

"Dwell in possibility."
– Emily Dickinson

Think about the people you trust.
Why do you trust them? Is it because they said *"Trust me"* or *"You can trust me"*? No, these people have proven themselves trustworthy by continually doing things in a way that has built our trust. They got to know us and are reliable.

In short, they earned our trust by ***"giving a hoot."*** Few people *give a hoot* these days. When you show genuine interest in others, it shines a big attractive spotlight on you as someone with whom to cultivate a relationship. We have all met people who are totally focused on themselves, their interests, and their goals.

Are they fun to talk to?
Can you rely on them?
Are they people you want to help?

It is, of course, vital to know where you want to go in life. But if you exclude others because of your self-absorption, you are actually slowing down your own progress. Work hard not to be egotistical or selfish. Work diligently to increase the number of people you actively support and who support you, this leads to true influence and connection.

Helping others to progress is the proverbial two-sided coin. It helps you to progress in equal measure.
It takes a series of progress-based impressions to travel the long road from met to net.

"One thing I've learned through all the ups and downs is that if you're doing things right, then you have a core group of people. Not just a core group like your homies or your buddies, but a group of people that has a good influence on you, who you respect and admire, and you know that if they're on your side, you're doing something right."
- Hope Solo

Find Dots, Make Dots, Connect Dots!

Making connections often requires assertiveness. Be a conversation starter. Some people find it easy to strike up conversations with strangers and keep track of old colleagues. For others, networking is a tough, mysterious, and largely neglected process. For most people, learning how to meet and talk with strangers isn't easy. But do not ignore strangers. ***I know what your parents said, but you must talk to strangers.***

A coaching client of mine had been trying for months to get a certain businessman to join him at a very active weekly networking event sponsored by his local Chamber of Commerce. Finally this man came to the event. He walked into the room packed with people. He looked at the pool of business professionals. Looked at my client and said, *"I don't know anyone here. I'm out of here!"* And he LEFT, literally turning his back on a roomful of opportunities.

When my client told me about his misguided friend, it reminded me of the classic story of the two shoe-sales professionals who were sent to sell shoes to the Aborigines. One sends a telegram back to headquarters reading,
"No opportunities here. No one is wearing shoes."

The other sends a telegram back that says,
"Plenty of opportunities here. No one is wearing shoes!"

It is all in how you look at it. You have to see strangers for what they are – opportunities. Plus, when you talk to strangers they stop being strangers. *They might still seem strange, but they're no longer strangers.*

At one point:
Bill Gates and Paul Allen were strangers.
You and your significant other were strangers.
Miles Davis and Charlie Parker were strangers.
Keith and Mick were strangers.
Oprah and Dr. Phil were strangers.
Sonny and Cher were strangers.
Those Google dudes were strangers.

It is safe to assume that most people are at least a tad nervous at networking functions. Help others get more comfortable by approaching them first. It is boring and close to a waste of time to attend a networking function and just stand around waiting for someone to come up to you and inquire about you. ***Take Action!***

"Behold the turtle. He makes progress only when he sticks his neck out."
-- James B. Conant

Commit yourself to proactively meeting new people. Be open to new ideas and opportunities. Find common interests. Find ways to help. Find connections, make connections and connect connections.

Find Dots.
Make Dots.
Connect Dots.

Be Progress.

The CONNECTION CODE

CODE Prospecting

The four letters that make up the word **CODE** stand for the four proven steps consistently taken by successful professionals to Build Powerful Connections, Gain Influence, Prospect Effectively and Win Sales:

Create Strong Belief in Self and Services

Open Face-to-Face Relationships

Deliver Solid First Impressions

Earn Trust

Quick note on: O – Open Face-to-Face Relationships:
As the former CMO of an award-winning digital marketing company, I believe in the awesome power and reach of Digital Marketing, Social Media and the Internet in general. With that said, we have a much better opportunity to make a solid positive connection when we meet people face to face. Fair enough?

"Keep your dreams alive. Understand to achieve anything requires faith and belief in yourself, vision, hard work, determination, and dedication. Remember all things are possible for those who believe."

- Gail Devers

The First – *and most vital* - Step to INFLUENCE and CONNECTION is to: ***Create Strong Belief in Self and Services.***

Before we make connections effectively, we must feel it is inevitable that we will meet and help people. We must feel it is inevitable that we will continue to progress. It simply will happen. It is happening. We will help other people reach their goals. We will reach our goals. We are progressing and we help others progress.

People pick up on that feeling. It's a buzz, an aura. It surrounds you. It's appealing. It draws the right people to you. Andra Grava, an extremely well-connected business owner and entrepreneur in my network, told me about a really interesting networking group called *Success North Dallas*, founded by Bill Wallace. One of their few criteria for membership in *Success North Dallas* is that you must ***"Be a Success in Your Own eyes.*** Be a success in your own eyes. That's what I'm talking about! We must radiate strong self confidence and belief in ourselves and our services.

You have to feel successful. Not Cocky or Uppity, just good about yourself.

We can't go into a networking moment looking for success. We have to take success with us into that networking moment. . Success breeds success. Success attracts success.

It is so important to feel successful. To believe you are progressing. To feel like a winner. Radiating strong belief in yourself and your services makes you attractive to be around. You ooze confidence. You create an aura of inevitability. You must believe you can help. That you *will* help. It is inevitable. It is vital to radiate belief in your self and your services.

Sometimes you are going to have to act more positive and confident than you feel. If you do, you will soon start to feel more positive and confident.

Change the negative perceptions about yourself and you will easily build greater trust and rapport with others.

"The greatest ability in business is to get along with others and to influence their actions."
- John Hancock

I know this is almost impossible to pull off, but try to compete only with yourself and do not compare yourself with others.

Our overriding goal is to be the best we can be for ourselves and others. Keep trying. **Progress does not demand perfection, only persistence.** And consider this: **Often what hinders our progress is not who we think we are, but who we think we can not become.**

Don't let anyone *(including yourself)* say you can not become someone with greater influence and connection. .

- *As a young student, Martin Luther King, Jr., was told by a teacher that he would never be able to speak with enough passion to motivate people into taking action.*

- *Thomas Edison was told by educators that he was too stupid to comprehend anything.*

- *Walt Disney was fired by a newspaper editor because he had "no good ideas."*

- *Beethoven's music instructor once said of him, "As a composer, he is hopeless."*

- *A magazine editor once informed Emily Dickinson that he could not publish her poems because they failed to rhyme.*

- *Michael Jordan was cut from his high school basketball team at the start of his sophomore year.*

Fear's for Suckers! One of the main reasons it is hard to meet new people and make connections effectively is **FEAR.**

Zig Ziglar often uses a popular acronym for fear. He says fear stands for: **False Evidence Appearing Real.** *Right on, Zig.*

To become truly fearless we must work daily to fear less. It *can* be intimidating to approach someone and start a conversation. Ralph Waldo Emerson knew the way around this universal fear, but most of all he knew the way *through* it: ***"Do the thing you fear and the death of fear is certain."***

Say it with me: ***Fear, you got nothing on me!***

Progress Agents get all the butterflies in their stomach to fly in formation and then soar above their comfort zone to a new, more expansive comfort zone. Progress Agents don't make making connections more complicated than they need to be.

Develop strong networking skills so you can make connections without being rattled and intimidated. **The more intimidated we are by the concept of connecting, the less effective we are in the process of connecting.**

Emerson's advice will help you overcome the fear of making connections with new people. Use Nike's formula and *Just Do It!* These new contacts may eventually become strategic partners, customers, employees, employers, or even best friends.

Remember, most people enjoy giving each other assistance, information, and advice. No one is getting voted off the island at the end of the event.

Really, do not be a Mumpsimus. No, that is not misspelled and no, I didn't call you a dirty word. Well, maybe I did – sort of. Mumpsimus (*pronounced MUMP-si-mus*) is a seldom-used word. I was introduced to it by Rick Loy, the Vice President of Sales for AdvoCare *(I highly recommend their SPARK drink).*

Mumpsimus means:

- *a person who persists in a mistaken expression or practice.*
- *an erroneous practice, use of language, or belief that is obstinately adhered to.*

In other words, the unfortunate state of mumpsimus means pigheaded adherence to a notion or expression that is popular but obviously wrong. Do not be a mumpsimus about business networking

Resist the popular notion that business networking is all fake sincerity and pushy behavior. That is just not so. Networking is not about arm-twisting.

It is not trying to get someone to do something that does not make sense for them to do. It is not the scary old backslapping sales shenanigans.

The simple fact is, most people are cool and want to meet you. You will not find Eeyore or Oscar the Grouch at most business networking events.

I do need to mention, though, that no matter how cool, giving, and funny you are, there are going to be some folks who just don't get it. They are not interested in anything or anybody, and are always bummed out.

My quick advice is: ***Move on.***

Do not let their flawed human thing rock you. Really, who can honestly say they enjoy talking to a negative blowhard? People like this expect the worst and that is exactly what they get. Somebody forgot to tell them that you create your own reality and if you expect bad stuff to happen, bad stuff happens.

You know the people I am talking about – the ones who look and act like they just ate a big steaming bowl of "Catcher in the Rye."

They're irritable, easily agitated, restless types who love a good argument. Chances are, they are not feeling too wonderful, either.

So what are the possible causes of soreheaditus?

- *Maybe their back is out of alignment. That could make you a sourpuss.*
- *Financial and personal problems can make you a bellyacher.*
- *Hating your job can make you crabby.*
- *A hangnail.*
- *Hunger.*
- *Perhaps it's Monday.*

So how come more people are not walking around scowling and biting the heads off of bats? (Maybe because bats are hard to catch?). I'll tell you the real reason. It's all in their attitude. Those disgruntled people CHOOSE their bummed reaction to the world because they do not know how else to deal with it.

They need a little Monty Python. They need to *"Always Look on the Bright Side of Life."*

Progress Agents have discovered that improving the way they look at things makes life easier in all aspects.

Think of Oscar the Grouch types as just nice people who have not yet been taught how to cope with life's stresses and challenging moments. Taking responsibility for themselves and their choices has never occurred to them before.

Maybe they grew up in a dysfunctional family and had no suitable role models to show them more appropriate ways of responding.

Progress Agents always set a good example for faultfinders to follow. ***Best to adopt the "live and help progress" philosophy,*** and never to be quick to make judgments.

Mumpsimus Revisited:
The generally accepted story of the word's origin is found in the 1517 writing of Richard Pace, a humanist and friend of Sir Thomas More. Pace later became the Dean of St Paul's Cathedral in London. Pace tells of a medieval monk who persisted in saying "quod in ore mumpsimus" instead of "quod in ore sumpsimus" when celebrating mass. "Sumpsimus" is Latin for "we have taken," and the full phrase translates to "which we have taken into the mouth." "Mumpsimus" is just babble.

It isn't clear whether the well-seasoned monk was illiterate (though that is the general assumption) or whether the word was transcribed incorrectly in his copy of the mass. What made this particular mistake memorable is that when a younger monk tried to correct the old guy, the older man replied that he had been saying it that way for over forty years and added, "I will not change my old mumpsimus for your new sumpsimus." And that is how 'mumpsimus' came to mean: A. a person who persists in a mistaken expression or practice. B. an erroneous practice, use of language, or belief that is obstinately adhered to. Not sure if you wanted to know, but now you do.

Your Mind Is a Terrible Thing to Use Against Yourself

Remember, you have good stuff to share. Like yourself – but never be cocky or vain. Like who you are on the *inside*. If you don't like yourself – *Big Problem.* Far too many people go around disliking themselves, focusing in on the negatives. This is a huge part of the reason why substance abuse, gambling, depression, anxiety, stress-related physical disorders, obesity, and other eating disorders are all galloping epidemics. Negative self-thoughts aren't just self-limiting, they can kill you.

Find a way to feel good about yourself. Hang with people who – like PBS's Mister Rogers – *"like you just the way you are."* Allow their views to rub off on you. Make yourself appealing to yourself. *Say it with me: I'm OK. You're OK.*

The expression OK started as kind of a joke. During the late 1830s, in newspapers around Boston, it was considered super funny to shorten a phrase to initials only and then supply an explanation in parentheses. Sometimes the abbreviations were misspelled to add to the humor. OK was used as an abbreviation for "all correct," the joke being that neither the O nor the K was correct. I'm All Correct. You're All Correct.

We each have a wealth of ideas, experiences, contacts, and resources that others need. Recognize and use these strengths of yours. Develop a healthy self-concept. I do not want to go all Dr. Phil on you, but you have to go inside before you can go outside.

We need to be real careful about what we say to ourselves and believe about ourselves. Henry Ford is quoted as saying "Whether you think you can or think you can't – you're right." Around the same time, Luigi Pirandello wrote a play that said the same thing: *Right You Are, If You Think You Are.*

Yes, I am talking about *affirmations.* When I realized that I was going to passionately encourage people to focus on affirmations, I admit I had nightmares of Stuart Smalley (Al Franken's character from "Saturday Night Live"): *"I'm good enough, I'm smart enough, and doggone it, people like me."*

Affirmations just seemed so wishy-washy, so flimsy. But I dug deeper and came to realize that we use affirmations all the time. It's just that most of them are negative and self-limiting:

"I have a short attention span."
"I am not good at meeting people."
"I am not a morning person."
"I participate in road rage."

Our brains are trippy and complicated and can do amazing things. But at their core our brains want one thing –*To Be Right.*

Whatever we continually say about ourselves and start to believe about ourselves, our brains are going to work to make it true.

It is imperative that we are careful with the things we say to ourselves because: *Whatever you say to yourself, you're right.*

"You got to fight for your mind
While you got the time."
-- Ben Harper

Try using self-empowering affirmations and visualizations to create a more positive attitude about yourself.

Stuff like:
"I believe in myself."
"I am always interested in connecting with new people."
"Things work out for me."
"I make good decisions that positively affect my life."
"This is a really good book."

Enjoy yourself. Mingle and keep it light. Go to business networking events *expecting* to have a positive experience. As with any business growth strategy: **If you think business networking is a bad idea, you will prove yourself RIGHT.**

Always act like an equal – because you are. Sure, some in the room make more money than you today, but real wealth is measured by what you are and not by how much you have. I know that sounds hokey, but it is still true.

You can act your way to better feelings, but rarely can you feel your way to better actions. Repetition is the mother of skill and competence.

Feelings follow actions and behavior.
Do not wait to make connections when you feel like it, or you may never get rolling. Far too many professionals never network enough to develop the confidence that comes with experience. They do not go through the *Met to Net* process enough to get comfortable.

Don't feel that you're good at conversation?
Ask great questions and listen.

Read for thirty minutes a day. Take in all the information you can. Read anything and everything so you can carry your share of the conversation.

Live in a hockey town? Read the hockey scores even if you don't know the meaning of a hat trick *(Google it).* Know you can pull your conversational weight.

Be a student of the universe. Knowledge about many issues and trends makes you more interesting. People coming in contact with you will more likely want to associate with you if you are well-read and knowledgeable.

Don't have time to read? Listen to books, speeches, and podcasts in your car or while exercising.

Bring the whole package to the party. How you look and what you wear matters, too. Perception counts. How you feel you look also has a big impact on how confident you will feel at the event.

People can pick up on how you feel about yourself, and whether you feel you have game. Dress and groom with care, knowing that what you wear conveys a message to others as well as to yourself.

Again, the easy healthy advice… Drink water, get enough sleep, eat healthy food *(whatever that is this week – I hear some veggies may still be good for you),* exercise, and watch your weight. I am not saying this stuff just because it will make you look better to the people you meet *(although that never hurts. We all must* take care of ourselves and eat right for countless reasons, here are two reasons:

A. We need to be proud of ourselves and how we look.

B. We need energy *(and not the quick sugar rush of a honey- glazed donut).*

We have strong belief in ourselves and our services when we have created the internal belief and commitment that we can and we will FIND ways to Be Progress for others.

Be a success in your own eyes.

Be Progress for all you meet.

"Be humble. You are made of earth.
Be noble. You are made of stars."
-- *Serbian proverb*

Making connections effectively is a skill. As with any skill, you will get better at it with practice. To network effectively, it is vital that you get over the stuff about meeting people that bothers you. If you're worried about having nothing to say or becoming tongue-tied, role-play with a friend until you feel more confident.

The more you exercise your connection muscles, the stronger they get and the easier networking becomes.

Networking is hard when you feel you HAVE to, and so easy when you feel you WANT to.

Attitudes are contagious.
Are yours worth catching?

Remember, making connections is as natural as eating and sleeping. We do it all the time. Whenever you talk with others and ask their opinions to help you make an informed decision – even if it's just to find a good book, CPA or dog groomer – you're networking. Networking is a vital quality-of-life skill that anyone can utilize to make more opportunities.

Meeting people is not really that tough, but connecting with people and making a great first impression is. Making a great first impression can be honed and perfected by practice. Practice on strangers – even that dude wearing flip-flops in front of you in line at Mickey D's. Elevators are good places for a chat.

Start striking up conversations with strangers in lines *(grocery store checkout, movie ticket, hot dog stand, etc.).* Make effective business networking a habit. Practice every day, every chance you get.

Remember, every contact enlarges your net and gets you closer to the people who could enrich your life or utilize your products and services.

"You gotta try your luck at least once a day, because you could be going around lucky all day and not even know it."
-- Jimmy Dean

Have a conversation and make a real connection with as many people as possible, get contact info and keep making contact. Keep in touch with those you wish to influence in an ever growing number of ways. . Communicate regularly with pivotal people in your industry and in other industries. Many have enormous power that could help you gain access to almost anyone, many of whom you could never reach on your own.

If you have support from these people, you will save yourself a lot of time and trouble in getting where you want to go. Doors will seem to magically fly open for you.

For our influence to grow,
Our foe is not the status quo ,
But our internal drive to gain access
To things we do not yet know.

Keep reaching out for you are only a few connections away from a great new opportunity!!!

Do you remember the Six Degrees of Kevin Bacon game? It was all the rage a few years back. The game is based on the main concept in John Guare's play *Six Degrees of Separation,* which was adapted into a movie with Will Smith.

The play theorizes that we are all connected by six or fewer stages of circumstance or acquaintance.

Six Degrees of Kevin Bacon takes this concept one step further (or back). Kevin Bacon has been in a ton of movies and many of them were ensemble films, like *Diner* and *Mystic River*. If you use Kevin as an end point, you can link him in six steps (degrees) or fewer to almost any other performer.

For example, Kevin Bacon links to John Lithgow in one quick classic link: Both were in *Footloose*. (1)

Kris Kristofferson, however, may take all six steps to make the chain. Let's see if I can make the steps using some of my all time favorite actors, actresses and films... Kris was in *A Star Is Born* with Barbra Streisand. (1) Barbra was in *The Way We Were* with Robert Redford. (2) Robert was in *Brubaker* with Morgan Freeman. (3) Morgan was in *Driving Miss Daisy* with Dan Ackroyd. (4) Dan was *in The Blues Brothers* with John Belushi. (5) John was in *Animal House* with Kevin Bacon. (6)

I'm sure you can get from Kris to Kevin in fewer moves, but I wanted to give an example of the full six degrees of separation.

Wildly Unimportant FYI:

I am linked to Kevin in two moves.
Dean was in TWISTER (Warner Brothers)
With Bill Paxton. (1) Bill was in Apollo 13
with Kevin Bacon. (2)

Yes, I was in TWISTER. *Don't blink.*
The flying cow ended up with a bigger part than I did.
I was one of the 'bad guys' driving the black vans.

There is so much I could share that is interesting
but not relevant to this topic. I will share this:
Bill Paxton was the coolest. Solid, fun, everyman-type
leader. Grade-A stuff. He made everyone around
him feel great. RIP Bill Paxton.

"Networking is all about connecting with people. But then again, isn't that what life is about?"

- Jay Samit

The Second Step to INFLUENCE and CONNECTION is to: ***Open Face-to-Face Relationships.***

The key is to create and stick to a business networking strategy. Proactively seek new connections. Develop your plan of action and get started without delay. Identify who you want to meet, where you are likely to meet them, and how you will follow up. Invest quality time thinking about the people who can best offer you the right information, contacts, and opportunities. Build relationships with these people by understanding what you have to offer them.

Where are the best places to make face-to-face contact with them?

Answering this question will help you decide which organizations you should belong to and which events you should attend. Important point: The organizations that are the best fit will change over time as your business grows and your career develops. Go with realistic expectations. You are (probably) not going to land a big account or forge an automatic *strong* link from a five-minute encounter. Making connections takes patience! Networking takes persistence! Come to terms with the fact that it is probably going to take more than one meeting for folks to come to the conclusion that you are amazingly with-it and that you offer progress for their lives.

In my research I have determined that it takes ***six to eight progress-based impressions*** to begin to solidify trust with a new person or organization.

Patience and Persistence! Keep firmly in your mind that business networking may not provide immediate financial benefits. It may take weeks -if not months or years -to see the full ripple of positive results of your business networking efforts, or you could open your e-mail in the morning and have a cool opportunity from someone you connected with the day before.

Shy? Nervous? *That's understandable.*
Start with people you know and trust. Share your desire to be introduced to quality individuals who would be good for you to know. Get connected to the people your contacts know.

Vary your activities. Grow your list of contacts each week. Start now and do not stop. If you're planning to hit several networking events in a single day, make sure you take time out to recharge. Plan your schedule so that you have periods of solitude. Guard against scheduling a full day of networking activities if you plan to network at an evening event. You're after quality, not quantity. As you and your network grow, you will need to make some changes. Let go of organizations and associations you can no longer maintain properly, or that are no longer relevant. Without forgetting where you came from, allow your network to evolve with you.

Best to keep your "smart phone" in your pocket while opening relationships. Resist!! Show self-discipline!! Just because the person you were speaking with gets pulled into another conversation doesn't mean it's time for you to check your Instagram feed. **Keep Connecting!** ***Keep Net-WORK-ing!***

Have a goal for each event. Decide what you hope to gain before you go. Write it down. Then get there and work toward it. Commit to staying until you have met and connected with your predetermined number or selection of people. Think about it. Set a target and push yourself. This will keep you from walking aimlessly around the room.

We progress by planning and performing, not by comparing and complaining.

Keep a log. For a month, keep a log of everyone you meet. Then classify and analyze them. Study your network!!

- *Which contacts are most valuable? Where did you meet them?*
- *Who are the takers and who are the givers?*
- *Any time-wasters?*
- Hey, your time is valuable too.

"The unsuccessful person is burdened by learning, and prefers to walk down familiar paths. Their distaste for learning stunts their growth and limits their influence"
- John C. Maxwell

The Most Important Thing to Carry With You is YOUR reason WHY

Before you get too far along in business networking, ask yourself these 37 questions. Your answers will guide you in making wise investments of your time, and help you build the most constructive relationships.

1. ***Why do you want a larger and/or better network of connections?***
2. ***What are your characteristics of a new high-quality connection?***
3. ***Are you looking for more business?***
4. ***What type of business?***
5. ***Who do you want to influence??***

Identify the gaps in your network. Maybe your network is limited to only knowing people in your particular industry. It is a big, continually growing, diverse business world out there and your network needs to reflect that.

6. ***Do you know too many people with similar backgrounds, or who think the same way?***
7. ***With whom do you need to build a relationship?***
8. ***Who can help you build your business or develop your career?***
9. ***Who are the people whose opinions are most valued in your industry?***
10. ***How can each person you identify contribute to your success?***
11. ***What can you do for these people so they will want to be in a relationship with you?***

12. *What do you have to offer them? What's in it for them?*
13. *Where will you find these people?*
14. *How will you arrange to meet them?*
15. *Who can offer an introduction to the people you wish to meet?*
16. *What will you say to them that will elicit their interest in you?*
17. *Why would anyone want to remember you?*
18. *How can you nurture the relationship?*
19. *How can you earn a place in their lives?*
20. *How likable are you?*
21. *How trustworthy?*
22. *Do you make a point of speaking well of others?*
23. *Are people right in thinking of you as an expert?*
24. *What are your priorities and objectives for a particular event?*
25. *Why do customers choose you or your business over your competitors?*
26. *How can you prove to others that they can rely on your word?*
27. *Are you known as someone who under-promises and over-delivers, or as one who over-promises and delivers squat?*
28. *What is the buzz or word-of-mouth about you?*
29. *What is the buzz about your company?*
30. *What is the buzz about your service?*
31. *When you accept an invitation to an event or party, do the hosts have doubts that you will actually show up?*
32. *Do you show up?*

33. ***How many people would stake their reputation on you?***
34. ***What are people saying about your work ethic?***
35. ***Who initiates most of your business or social conversations?***

Look, if others are not striking up conversations with you or inviting you out, this might be saying something about you and how you are perceived.

Finally, always ask yourself these two basic questions when going to any networking event. Remember to focus on finding the answers while at the function.

36. ***How can I make events I attend more beneficial for others?***
37. ***How can I benefit each person I meet?***

Sometimes it may appear one-sided, but in the world of networking - What Goes Around, Comes Around.

"No one is dumb who is curious. The people who don't ask questions remain clueless throughout their lives."
- Neil deGrasse Tyson

Making Connections

We can and should open relationships everywhere. To make connecting easier and more focused, look for groups and events where networking is encouraged. People expect to exchange contact information and meet new people at these types of gatherings, so go expecting to make some solid connections.

It is best not to consider joining any business organizations unless you are committed to being an *active member* for at least one year.

Effective networking takes patience and persistence.

Too many people go to business networking events with the wrong focus and try to force their service down your throat. If you are not on the top of your game, you will end up stoically listening to a bunch of pitches instead of getting the person to have a real conversation.

Also, it is possible to spend a bunch of dinero on joining networking groups, so consider your affiliations carefully. Call and ask if you can attend as a visitor. Most allow at least one free visit.

Again, you SHOULD network everywhere and anywhere. There are many places that offer networking possibilities. What follows is by no means a complete list, but these suggestions can lead to other opportunities.

17 Examples of Proven Places to Make Connections Effectively:

1. Organizations to Which You Already Belong
The first place to start networking is in the organizations you already belong to. Anywhere you are already connected: your homeowners' association, office parties, Sunday school class, PTA, workout club, sports groups, political party meetings, Junior League. Anywhere.

2. Professional and Trade Associations
Your professional trade association can put you in touch with colleagues in your field. Cultivate relationships with other members, tap into their expertise, discuss industry concerns, and swap ideas. These are usually the best organizations for gaining fresh insight into your industry, your clients, and *your competition*.

Check out your membership directory to find experts in the profession. Contact them for advice or ideas. The sooner you get involved in your trade association, the sooner your name will get out there. Serve on committees, contribute articles to the group's publications, speak at conferences, run for the board. Learn and practice new skills at educational seminars. You can learn how to use emerging technologies and catch up on new techniques. Read the association's newsletter for tips on how to succeed and use the full benefits of membership. Contact supplier members. They can tell you about new products and services used in your industry.

3. State and National Trade Shows, Conventions, and Conferences

Business and industry trade shows, conventions, and conferences have great potential as really solid places to network. However, a bewildering number of people never take advantage of these solid opportunities even when they go, because they treat the trip as a much deserved paid vacation instead of one of the best spots in the cosmos to make new contacts. This is not the place to let your hair down and get your groove on. Some of the big trade shows draw participants from around the globe. So much potential! At breakfast, lunch, dinner, and networking activities, meet as many people as possible, get their cards and stay in touch. Study the schedule and ask the organizers for a list of attendees before you go. Formulate a plan to make it a valuable investment of time and money.

At conventions, try contacting keynoters and concurrent-session presenters ahead of time. *Most often we speakers are from out of town and do not know anyone, so invite us to sit with you during lunch, or schedule time for a cup of coffee.* At least introduce yourself to the presenters and those sitting around you.

4. Trade Organizations of Your Best Customers

If the fine people who already use your services belong to these organizations, would it not be safe to assume that other members might want to use your services as well? See if you can present a breakout session or seminar on something related to your work.

5. Chamber of Commerce
They don't call them Chambers of Commerce for nothing. More than likely, your community's Chamber of Commerce is in the position to serve as your greatest local establishment for making priceless business relationships, but only if you're active and informed.

Most Chambers welcome guests at functions but are usually only interested in recommending their members. The upside is that you can join as a business or as an individual. Chambers sponsor networking activities like after-hours mixers, business-networking breakfasts, luncheons, and even leads groups. Chamber events are great forums for sharpening your skills and opening face-to-face relationships.

6. Organizations that Share Your Philosophy
If you care about the purpose of the organization, you will be proud to be a member and reap personal satisfaction, along with the opportunity to build relationships. Get involved in a charity that feels right.

7. Small Business Development Centers - SBDC
Most metropolitan areas have a couple of SBDCs. Whether you have your own business or are an employee, these business centers offer courses and resources to help you to grow and meet people.

8. Golf / Sports
Golf has long been *the* sport for business networking. So if you're a somewhat decent swinger, tee up. Other sports work fine for networking, too. The key is to find a sport you are interested in, and get involved.

9. Hobby/Passion

Join groups that offer possibilities for making contacts and achieving personal growth: art appreciation, dancing, chess, astronomy, wine and food clubs, etc. You will meet others with similar interests who are ready to network. Go to meetings that feature discussions on a topic you're interested in.

10. Spiritual Organizations

I am NOT suggesting that you join a church or synagogue only for the business opportunities. But let's face it – many solid business relationships are forged in the pews and folding chairs of spiritual organizations. Go for the right reasons and let your light shine. *Hide it under a bushel?* No. You've got to let it shine.

11. College Associations

Having common backgrounds makes for easy conversations and many really get a kick out of helping an alum of their university.

12. Workshops, Classes, and Seminars

Take every chance to learn more and make yourself better. Other people committed to jogging the road to success will be there too. Contribute ideas. Ask questions.

13. Cultural Events

Meet some people with style and taste. Theater, symphony, art exhibits, rodeos, tractor pulls…

14. Leads Groups
The great thing about leads groups is that they are focused on lead generation for their members. Expect events held by leads groups to be more intense than the rest of the networking options on this list. Make sure you check out the membership roster before you join. If there are some members who are in your line of work, you will probably want to join another leads group. They may not even let you join if there is already someone in your category. Also, find out what the member obligations are, and ask some of the members how much business they have generated from being a member.

15. Kiwanis, Rotary, AMBUCS, Lions, Elks, Moose
(I know there is an animal joke in there somewhere.)
Doing good for the community in service organizations while you are building connections is a rock-solid plan. *Here it really pays to serve as a leader.*

16. Connect and Re-Connect Using the Internet!!
-- *Heard of this thing called the internet?* -- Having served for several years as the Chief Marketing Officer for Synclab Media, an award-winning digital marketing company, I am a firm believer in the amazing power of the *fast moving and ever-evolving World Wide Web.*

However, any specific insights or tips shared in this Handbook on using *Twitter, LinkedIn, Facebook, Instagram, or Snapchat* would soon be outdated.
I will share this Progress Agent Marketing Truth:
Whether connecting face-to-face *or online,* it takes *a Series of Progress-Based Impressions* to Grow Influence and Connection.

17. Volunteer / Get Active

A great way to gain visibility and develop relationships is through volunteering with any of the above-listed groups. Almost all these groups could use a hand. Step out and step up. Look for volunteer jobs that will provide you opportunities to show off your skills and personality, and meet and interact with new contacts. You increase your impact as well as the potential for new contacts when you actively participate.

Volunteer to:

- Chair a Committee, Run for Office, Join the Board. You will connect with key industry leaders and gain a reputation as a leader yourself. Let people experience your leadership, communication, and organizational skills in action.

- Serve on a Committees. You can help shape the association's policy, as well as work closely with and learn from other experts.

- Work the Reception Desk. You will meet people as they sign in.

- Be a *People Mover* and direct people to the right rooms at a large conventions,

- Be a Greeter. The greeter spot is ideal for the self-diagnosed shy, because the title alone forces you to connect. Plus, as a greeter there is an automatic assumption that you are "in the know" and others will naturally come to you for info and help.

Fifteen Progress Agent Handbook Strategies for Making Face-to-Face Connections

Here are fifteen proven strategies for making a connection at business networking events.

1. Know as much as you can about the attendees.
Research the people you want to meet. Before the event, ask the sponsors of the event for a list of attendees and create your most- wanted "hit list" of people you definitely want to connect with. When calling organizers to RSVP for an event, ask for information about people in your focus market or VIPs who might be attending. That way, you will have two or three people in mind who you would like to meet when you arrive.

2. Go it alone.
When attending networking functions, go by yourself or at least communicate to your carpool buddies that you should all fan out. Moving about a networking event solo encourages people to approach you and makes it easy to mingle and initiate conversations. It may be more comfortable to have a friend right there with you, but remember: you are there to grow your network, not hang with the people already in your network.

3. Look for people standing alone.
These folks may be nervous, and your initiative will often endear you to them. Plus, one-on-one networking is the best networking.
It is hard to join a group unless invited.

4. Get an introduction to the person you want to meet.

An introduction is an implied endorsement. Try to get introduced by the most respected person at the event with whom you have a relationship. The influential business networkers are always happy to play a part in your success and you look like a winner by association.

Who are the people who have established a good reputation? Who loves to network and knows a lot of people?

These people have a large circle of influence and understand the power of networking. They are quick to bond and make the most of relationships. *(Be sure to ask them if there is someone you can introduce them to.)*

Who are the most influential connections inside your network?

Find out what they do. Study the techniques of the influential professionals in your network. Try to tag along with a well-connected person in your network to some of their normal networking functions and ask them to introduce you to a few of their contacts.

Give them some insight and direction by letting them know the kind of person you want to make a connection with – the more specific the better.

A slight modification on the same strategy
Look for someone you know who is chatting with a couple of people you do not know. Approach the group and stand to the side within view of the person you know. This serves as a subtle cue for your contact to introduce you to the group and bring you into the conversation. *Try it. It works.* If someone invites you to join the group but forgets to introduce you, take the initiative and introduce yourself.

"When the character of a man is not clear to you, look at his friends."
-- Japanese Proverb

5. Study the tags.
If nametags are preprinted and on display at the registration table, scan the tags of the other attendees to see what opportunities await you.

Though I have not tried this myself, Rachel Wood, a top financial advisor in the Boston area who introduced herself to me after one of my seminars on networking, does something interesting. If she spots a nametag on the registration table of someone she would like to meet, she asks the people manning the table if she can clip a note to their tag saying she would like to meet them. She swears by it.

By the way:
Leave your ego there at the registration desk. The first positive impression is the most important, and lays the groundwork for all future impressions. You want to make sure you are making a good one.

6. Circle and scan.
Before diving into the event, try circling the room and checking out the nametags for people or companies you definitely want to make contact with while there.

7. Sit between people you do not know well.
If the event is a sit-down affair, **do not sit by a friend or business associate.** You already know that person! You might be sitting there a while, so make sure you are going to be sitting by someone you can form a *new* relationship with. Plan who you want to sit by, but wait until the last minute to actually sit down so you can keep making new contacts.

8. Hang out at the food table.
I know it sounds like I'm joking, but people tend to be easily accessible around food. Stand near the food table, but not the bar. People tend to grab their drinks and move away from the bar, but are more likely to linger near the grub.

As people check out the buffet table, small talk comes more easily. "That Danish looks good..." is as good an opener as any. Once they have their hands full, people often look for a flat surface where they can place their plate and beverage. Take a spot next to them and get to chatting.

Check this out.
Our endorphin levels are higher when we are close to food, which boosts our memory and the chance that we will remember and be remembered. *We humans are a trip, aren't we?*

"If more of us valued food and cheer and song above hoarded gold, it would be a merrier world."
-- JRR Tolkien

Do not go to networking functions hungry.
Eat before you go so you can focus on the person, not the cantaloupe. If you are hungry, grab a quick bite off to the side, and then mingle. Do not talk with your mouth full. *(I hope I didn't need to write that.)*

9. Stand near the registration table.
After you have registered and put on your nametag, take advantage of the many opportunities to make small talk with new arrivals after they have signed in. These are the couple of minutes when most people are alone and interested in someone new to communicate with.

Even something really easygoing like, "Looks like a good turnout..." is probably good enough to get a friendly conversation started. Remember that like you, people are there to make new contacts. And if they are not, they are in the wrong place.

10. Help others become more effective networkers.
Offer proven strategies and techniques for effective self-marketing and relationship-building. As your contacts' networks grow and strengthen, so do yours.

11. Speak at conferences.
Speaking in public strikes big fear in the hearts and minds of the unprepared. It is the #1 fear for a lot of people, one slot above death. But speaking has the power to position you as an expert, a leader, a thinker in your community and your industry.

Join Toastmasters (www.toastmasters.org) to get over the fear and polish the tools needed to become a confident speaker and a successful networker. Toastmasters can help you become an interesting person and a valuable resource to others by sharpening your communications skills. You'll gain self-confidence and learn to present a great first impression. Get ready, because with Toastmasters there are live speaking opportunities from the get-go.

12. Follow your money.
Who are your suppliers?
Where do you spend money?
What places do you frequent?

Get to know your vendors better. If you are their customer, they probably serve other topnotch business professionals like you, right? Find out who else they know. Their contacts could be worth more than the service or products they provide. Work to build the exchange of contacts into the relationships.
Ask them to recommend you. A nifty by-product of relationship-building is you will likely improve the quality of your service.

13. Include your friends and neighbors.
Far too often, we already know people with the right contacts or expertise, but we do not know it. It is imperative to get to know everyone in your existing network on a more solid footing.

Find out who your closest friends and colleagues know. It is probably worthwhile for you to get to know more of your friends' friends and your neighbors' neighbors (of course, you are first going to have to actually meet your neighbors). You never know where your next opportunity, job, or client will come from, so do not rule out your friends and relatives as possible contacts. Your Uncle Abbott may have a neighbor who has a son who needs exactly what your company has to offer.

"The greatest good we can do for others is not to share our riches, but to assist in revealing their own."
-- *Benjamin Disraeli*

14. Hug a "gatekeeper."
Make friends with the executive assistants of those you want to create a relationship with. Executive assistants can become solid allies or your worst nightmare. Do not make the mistake of taking them for granted or seeing them as obstacles to be overcome. Heck, they're the ones who set up appointments for the decision maker. And in a lot of cases...THEY *ARE* THE DECISION MAKERS. Get to know everyone in the office as individuals. Talk with them. Learn all the front-office folks' names, special interests and hobbies, the names of their kids, and stuff like that. Check for clues from what they display on their desks.

Be dependable and genuine. If you can build a solid bond with these key individuals, you will differentiate yourself from run-of-the-mill sales punks who ignore gatekeepers and just try to barge in to see the big chief.

If gatekeepers know and respect you, they can recommend you when the need for your service arises. They can keep you in the loop. They can be your greatest champion. Plus, executives respect you more if you have an authentic interest in their whole staff. Most executives like and respect their assistants and value their insight, so if the assistant likes you, so will the person in charge.

To gain a possible inside track, ask assistants what groups their boss is active in. Join those groups and get involved. When decision makers see you engaged in activities outside of the office, they develop more confidence and respect for you. *That's good.*

15. Bond with the spouses and significant others of the influential.

The influence and power wielded by spouses and significant others is grossly underestimated. And because of this, they often go ignored. When offered the chance at a function invest the time to make a solid connection with them. Get to know them as people, and after the event they are likely to speak well of you to the very person you targeted.

“This is important: to get to know people, listen, expand the circle of ideas. The world is crisscrossed by roads that come closer together and move apart, but the important thing is that they lead towards the Good.”

- Pope Francis

The Third Step to
CONNECTION & INFLUENCE is to:
Deliver Solid First Impressions.

Listen as if Your Lifestyle Depended on It. ***It Does!*** Everyone has a need to talk and be heard. Treat others as if they are the most important people on the planet because – in their minds – they are. Everyone wants to feel that they are significant and have meaningful ideas to share. Those who choose to really listen will always have someone to talk with. Notice that I wrote talk with, not talk to. The key is to:

Turn people ON to you by tuning IN to them.

Good listeners absorb and reflect on what they hear. They are active in the listening process. This requires energy and motivation because listening is more than just hearing. We must become active listeners rather than passive hearers.

Often our motivation to actively listen is not all that high. We think we can get by without really focusing. This is a mistake. The ability to value what others say is critical to building priceless relationships. To make solid first impressions, be determined to understand completely what others are trying to communicate.

"No man ever listened himself out of a job."
-- *Calvin Coolidge*

Collect your thoughts and focus. Think only about the present conversation. How often do you catch yourself thinking about some unrelated issue when you should be listening? It is difficult to *tune in* when you're preoccupied with previous conversations or unfinished tasks.

Business philosopher Jim Rohn is quoted as saying, "One of the greatest gifts you can give anyone is the gift of your attention." Rohn is right.

Don't get distracted by other people's nearby conversations.
If you have to, walk the person you are speaking with to a quieter place in the room to have your initial chat.

Try this. **Look directly at the person and when they stop speaking, count to two *(in your mind!)* before you speak.**

Committing to this brief pause:
A. helps you avoid interrupting the other person, who may have only paused to gather his or her thoughts.
B. establishes that what has just been shared was worth contemplation.
C. gives your brain time to digest the information and ask a good clarifying question or make a comment.

Good clarifying questions offer the person the chance to rephrase their thoughts and say precisely what they mean. Repeating back (as questions or tentative statements) what you think you've heard the other person say also makes people feel wonderful, and it avoids mind-misreading errors.

If making new connections stresses you out, you may turn into an overanxious talker and end up overpowering the fine folks in the dialogue and not letting anyone else talk. Active listening can help prevent this from happening. Think about it:

In the past, at the end of a conversation, did you tend to know more about the person, or did they learn more about you?

Discipline yourself to uttering no more than four sentences in a row without stopping. This ensures that others will have the opportunity to express themselves.

Two ears, one mouth. You know the saying.

"To listen well is as powerful a means of communication and influence as to talk well."
-- *John Marshall*

Ask Questions to Find NEXT STEP.

When making a new connection, **do NOT hog the conversation and start talking about yourself, your business, how cool you are, or your ideal prospect.**

A much better choice is to invest the lion's share of the discussion asking questions about that person and their business. *Find out what progress means to them.*

You make a much more powerful impression, a much more memorable impression, ***being interested in others*** rather than trying to *be interesting to others.*

This should ease your mind and help you relax because now the pressure is off. All you have to do is work to answer these questions.

What is most important to that person at this moment?

What can I do to help this person progress?

Start by asking the person you are chatting with Who, What, Where, Why and How kinds of questions.

> **"The wise man is not the one who gives you the right answers, but the right questions."**
> *-- Claude Levi-Strauss*

People want and need to talk about THEIR business, NOT YOURS. That's cool – encourage them. It gets you valuable follow-up info and saves you from having to come up with something witty. Just listen and ask questions relating to what they say and people will think you ROCK.

Always be thinking: *How can I help this person progress toward his or her goals?*
Give direct eye contact and be totally focused on trying to get to know the other person better. People like to talk about how they got to where they are.

The more rapport you have with an individual, the more receptive they will be to establishing a relationship with you. Ask conversational questions that bring out the contact's uniqueness. Listen carefully and concentrate on what the person is saying.

Get curious. It makes no sense to ask questions if you are not interested in the answers.

> **"The cure for boredom is curiosity. There is no cure for curiosity."**
> -- *Dorothy Parker*

These answers should make it easier to make positive impressions in the future. People love to talk about themselves, so master the art of asking questions and listening to the responses so you can ask relevant questions. If you can help them with a tidbit of information or link them to a resource, you will be seen as a caring and knowledgeable person.
You can either make a suggestion related to what their needs are, or help them in some other way. The person will remember that you were able to help them out.

Plus you will gain knowledge. **Knowledge is the key to power, and asking questions is seeking the keys to that power.** Asking people questions about themselves also makes you stand out in a positive way in their mind.

I have done a lot of interviews with business leaders and visionaries and have found that longer pauses before questions lead to longer answers. Taking these pauses makes you look professional and like you are really thinking and engaged, rather than just filling empty airtime.

It's okeydokey to script your questions. Just rehearse them enough so they don't sound scripted.

Here are eight solid questions and statements for starting conversations and delivering solid first impressions:

1. *How did you get into your line of work?*
2. *What interested you about the profession?*
3. *What do you like most about your industry?*
4. *What has been happening in your industry?*
5. *What are the current trends?*
6. *What have you found to be the best way of getting the word out and promoting your business?*

Also add these to your conversational Rolodex:

- *Tell me more.*
- *Please elaborate.*
- *What are your ideas about…?*
- *There is something I would like to ask you…*
- *What is your opinion on…?*

Do not ask questions in rapid-fire succession. This is not a Dragnet interrogation or a time for cross-examination. Nor is it a time to relive your glory days on the debate team. Avoid asking questions that are manipulative, boring, embarrassing, hostile, confrontational, insulting, or too intimate.

When you approach people, they will start talking about something, so follow that with them and go with the flow. Abrupt changes in conversational course cause confusion and frustration.

Every question you ask makes a statement about you. Only ask questions that make you look good (smart, concerned, with-it, etc.).

21 Progress Agent Handbook Tips for Delivering Solid First Impressions

Building a relationship entails a series of impressions that align us with a new contact. None is more important than the first. Make sure your first meeting with someone is powerful. Remember, people meet people all the time. You need to stand out as someone they want future contact with. *Here are 21 Progress Agent Handbook tips for delivering solid first impressions.*

1. Do not try to do major business deals (save that for later). Do not rush new relationships; think LONG TERM. Do not SELL! It is a mind-set. Be subtle. The worst thing you could do is try to start selling someone as soon as you meet them.

2. Be an Early Bird and a Late Bloomer.
Never be late. At a networking event the ten minutes before things get under way and the ten minutes after are the real golden moments. So arrive 15 minutes early and stay 15 minutes late.

3. Always stand when meeting someone new.
It shows respect. *What else can I say about it?*

4. Get revved up.
The most influential influence themselves first.
If you want people to have a positive feeling toward you, first create this emotion within yourself.
Everyone is, at some level, nervous about meeting new people. It is common to tense up when you are about to walk into a networking group.

Do whatever it takes to get yourself revved up and at the same time calm your nerves before the event. Try these to help get you straight *(somewhere you won't look stupid):*

- *Listen to educational and/or motivational speeches or your favorite music – loud – in your car. If you feel like it, sing along.*
- *Long Breath In… Do simple breathing exercises: Breathe in slowly for the count of ten, hold in breath, and breathe out slowly for the count of ten. Do this Five to Ten times.*
- *Stretch out your jaw (to avoid clenching your teeth).and Roll your shoulders.*
- *Clap your hands, Stretch and Shake it out!*
- ***Be ready to keep from having to get ready!***

5. Look them in the eyes.

You do not want to stare at them but you do need to look people in the eyes if you want them to start trusting you. If you find it difficult to offer or establish direct eye contact, challenge yourself to know what color the person's eyes are by the time you have asked your second question.

6. Catch that name.

We say we *forget* names. But I don't think that's true. I don't think we really *hear* the name of the person when we meet them. We are not listening. We are more focused on what we're about to say.

The other person's name is way important to them, probably about as important as yours is to you.

To make a great first impression, make a point of *catching* and *tossing around* the person's name in conversation. This is almost impossible when we are preoccupied with what we are going to do or say next to be impressive.

The Name Game

- Right before you meet new people, PREPARE to CATCH their name.
- Toss their name back in your first or second response.
- Mention their name naturally throughout the conversation (but do not overdo it).
- Repeat their name when parting.

If you do not catch it, ask them to repeat it rather than letting it go. Do not be embarrassed to ask *(they probably did not catch your name either).* Read others' nametags. That's what they're there for.

Again, your new contact's name is the ultimate word to use in order to make a solid first impression. Using the person's name in a natural manner throughout the conversation is an easy and organic way to create a memorable link between yourself and your new contact.

7. Hand in hand.
In the business arena, handshakes are the accepted greeting. As a rule, I would advise against initiating kisses or hugs in a business setting. Take the handshake seriously; you *will* be judged by the quality (limp/firm, moist/dry, lengthy/brief) of your handshake.

Above all, a handshake should be firm, *but not bone-crushing*. No dead fish handshakes. They're creepy.

Note to men about shaking hands with women:
Don't wimp out on the handshake. I often hear from female professionals I am working with how some men will offer them a lame *"I don't want to hurt you – you delicate flower, you"* handshake. Be a man.
Shake the hand.

You can avoid delivering a cold, wet handshake by keeping your drink in the left hand. If your hands tend to be clammy, try spraying them with antiperspirant at least once a day. Also, try carrying Kleenex in your pocket and drying your hands discreetly from time to time. To really put yourself over the top, shake hands good-bye as well as hello.

8. Travel light.
In most cases, there is no need to take your briefcase or even a purse. You do not want to have to put down all that stuff (brochures, briefcases, or handbags) and dig out a business card. It's also tougher to move around or look comfortable and easygoing with your arms filled with your company's propaganda. Remember, you are mostly there to connect, not sell.

9. Meet. Talk. Get card. Go.
At a networking event, talk to one person for about four to five minutes – eight minutes maximum. Get their card, take some notes, and work toward a comfortable conclusion to this initial conversation. Hogging someone's time is an inexcusable no-no. If you cannot find a natural way to end the conversation, introduce the person to someone else. It's a win-win. You help them connect with someone new and you get to move on without appearing rude.

10. Wear your nametag *(on your right side).*
Always wear a nametag at networking functions. This makes you easily accessible. Think of it as a sticky advertisement.

The reason you wear it on the right is that when you shake hands with your right hand your nametag is easy to read. During a handshake, the right shoulder moves in with the outstretched hand creating a line.
The receiver's eyes follow the line and wearing your nametag on the right side helps the other person find it easily. *Right is Right.*

If you are a longhaired woman *(or man for that matter),* be sure your hair does not cover your tag. If you have a company nametag – wear it. This indicates that you are serious about your career and not just passing through this position on the way to becoming a hermit or something. No company nametag? Take a thick black marker to write your name on the name badge.

11. Do not act desperate for business.
People want to talk to upbeat, confident people. You will not create any priceless business relationships if you act like you don't have lunch money. Treat people as worthy of your respect and courtesy, not as targets.

12. Carry /use breath mints or those dissolving strip things (not gum). Halitosis is bad for business. Good breath is a must. And as for gum, smacking anything at a networking function is discouraged.

13. Beware of the "Mound o' Stuff."
At many networking functions put on by Chambers of Commerce and the like, it is common to be able to put a flyer or brochure on everyone's chair prior to the event. Often when participants get to their chair, there is literally half an inch of business cards, flyers, four-color brochures, Hershey's kisses, candy canes (during the holidays) and a hodgepodge of promotional knickknacks needing to be moved out of the way so they can sit down.

Putting something on everyone's chair can be worthwhile. It can also be a HUGE waste of time and money. Rest assured, every trash bin within a hundred-yard radius will be overflowing with this stuff after the event, and most people do not even take the time to dig through the chair-mound.

Why should they?

What's in it for them?

If you put something on every chair, make it inexpensive, memorable, useful, or include a call to action – like a pen, a little calendar, or a special flyer featuring a really cool time-sensitive offer. No business cards or four-color brochures. A business card should be a personal hand-off presented via a face-to-face handshake. Those jazzy color brochures are way too expensive. *It is too much.*

If you have something worthwhile, make sure you get there early to distribute your items before participants start arriving. Nothing says "I do not have my stuff together" like trying to pass around your discount coupon after most people have already taken a seat.

Keep one of your items on hand and put the rest in your car or out of the way. When it is your time to do your "Rise and Shine" (addressed on pages 138-141), hold up the item and explain why it is worth their time to hunt through the mound for it.

Try a special drawing where you put a couple of dots on a couple of your flyers. Everyone has to look for your flyer to see if they have a dot. If they have one, they win something cool.

14. Respect the person's time.
Someone important to you is important to others. Strike up an engaging, unique conversation, learn something about them, make a solid impression, get their card, and excuse yourself at the appropriate moment. This will create a solid and classy first impression.

15. Pretend you are the host or hostess.
Introducing people you meet to others whom they may have something in common with earns big points. If you meet someone who is new to the event or a new member of the organization, answer their questions and then look around for someone who may be good for them to know. This keeps you moving and positions you as someone interested in helping others. When in doubt as to how a person wants to be introduced, use last names only.

16. Always keep it positive.

New Someone: *How are you?*
You: *I am great. How are you?*
New Someone: *How is business?*
You: *Rocking along. We're getting a lot of quality referrals.*
New Someone: *How do you like the weather?*
You: *Oh, I love rain.*

You get my point. Keep it positive. Do not be a whiner. Do not be an Eeyore or an Oscar the Grouch. No one wants to listen to complaining, fault-finding, or snooty attitudes.

17. Communicate that your network rocks.
Talk enthusiastically about the cool, neat, highly productive and witty people who are already in your network. This will encourage others to want to be in your network too, because you will speak of them in the same positive way.

18. Do not talk negatively about others *(especially competitors).*

Others will realize, if you speak badly to them about others behind their back, that you may also speak poorly of them when they are not around. Talking bad about competitors makes you look shallow and weak, and puts the focus on them instead of you. Plus, if you speak ill of someone, it will probably get back to them and start some unhealthy and unprofitable competition.

19. Do NOT air dirty laundry in public.

I was at a networking function where a guy used his time in front of the group to show us a three-ring binder he had created full of his negative correspondence with a certain local business owner. It was a major downer. Then he passed the three-ring binder around. This created a really weird negative vibe and discouraged me from wanting to build a real solid relationship with him. *What if he starts three-ring binders on everybody?*

20. Beware of Alcohol.

At conferences, conventions, trade shows, and business-after-hours functions *(often organized by the local Chamber of Commerce and held at a local business establishment),* it is common for there to be alcohol. **I encourage you to consider not drinking at these events,** *or at least know your alcohol limit and not get anywhere close to it.* Sure, you want to be remembered, but not as the loud jerk who couldn't hold his liquor and spilt red wine on Judge Jacob's new power suit.

21. The Rise and Shine:
Designing Your Classic 30-Second Commercial

At many business networking meetings, participants are given the opportunity to participate in what I call the **Rise and Shine**. This is usually a 30-second opportunity to *rise* from your chair and present yourself and what progress you offer through your business in a very concise, direct, and hopefully memorable way. This is your time to *shine.* You also benefit from hearing other participants give their promotional spot.

Do not use this time to brag. Egotism is boring. Focus on how you *help* others solve problems. *How are you providing progress?*

Here is a tried and true outline to follow:

My name is *(your name).*
I work with *(or run)* a company called *(your company).* We work with people *(or organizations)* who are ready to *(attract new customers, get their books in order, hire the right people, etc.)* so they can *(make more money, save time, be more productive, etc.),* because everyone can use more *(money, time, productivity, etc.). (Your name)* with *(your company).*

Important Related Tip:
Do not hold stuff in your hands when you do your Rise and Shine unless you are going to refer to it. It pulls focus away from you.

When meeting someone one-on-one, you have far less than the 30 seconds in a Rise and Shine to grab their attention. Come up with some progress-based statements that share your expertise and what you and your company offer in a clear, engaging way. If you talk aimlessly or just throw some stuff together on the fly, you will quickly lose their interest.

Always speak about what you do in a professional, positive manner. Concentrate on how others benefit from the product or service you perform.

It's important to communicate what you do in ways that will help the person you're speaking with understand that you provide solutions. They must have you positioned in their mind as an agent of progress.

Positioning revolves around quickly and clearly articulating who you work with, what problems you solve, what benefits you offer, and what results you produce.

A solid way to relate this is to communicate a common problem, followed by the solution you provide. This approach works because most people are totally immersed in their own challenges 24/7.

Problem/Solution Example: Debt Consolidator:
You know how a lot of people are drowning in debt and struggling to make ends meet?
I offer a service that helps people gain control of their finances and their future.

It is the benefit people want to hear about, not what you do. These statements need to become so automatic that you don't even think of them in terms of networking.

Stuff like:
I solve...
We save companies...
I help people...
We give ...
I make...
We design...
I teach the disorganized how to...

Avoid using your label as your introduction.
"I'm a CPA."
"I'm a massage therapist."
"I'm a car salesman."

Chances are, when you open with your label,
if you get a continued conversation,
that person is only being polite.

If you are a real estate agent: Say you assist people in finding their new Home Sweet Home.

If you are a stockbroker: Say you help people create wealth, financial independence, and peace of mind.

CPA: You do not do taxes. Heck, you're in the stress-reduction business.

If it fits your personality and service, it can be extremely profitable to come up with a hook or a catchy tag line that creates curiosity. These statements are memorable and start a conversation.

A great one that comes to mind is from *Doug Trumbull,* the owner of **Mighty Clean Carpet Cleaners** in *Plano, Texas:*

If it isn't Mighty Clean,
it's a dirty shame.

Another good one I heard recently is from a pest-control company *(specializing in getting rid of termites)* in Providence, Rhode Island:

Without Griggs & Browne,
the whole town would fall down.

"Sometimes, idealistic people are put off the whole business of networking as something tainted by flattery and the pursuit of selfish advantage. But virtue in obscurity is rewarded only in Heaven. To succeed in this world you have to be known to people."

- Sonia Sotomayor

The Fourth Step to INFLUENCE and Connection is to: **Earn Trust.**

Trust is the basis for all long-term relationships, even the one we have with ourselves. You may not believe this, but meeting people and making a solid first impression is the easy part. Earning their trust is more challenging. Earning their trust takes a series of Progress-based Impressions.

So keep it up. Keep on keeping on being progress. Keep making great impressions. This is why getting to know people and their interests during the first conversation is so important. The more you know about them – their lives, their goals – the more ways you can help them progress and earn their trust. Think of getting to know others as doing individual market research.

"Most good relationships are built on mutual trust and respect."
- Mona Sutphen

As Captain D. Michael Abrashoff, former commander of the *USS Benfold*, relates in his book, *It's Your Ship*, ***Trust makes money.*** Trust is the basis for profitable long-term relationships. Building trust takes time. Trust is the promise of progress.

Trust is fragile and can be weakened by broken promises and unrealistic expectations. So mean what you say and do what you say you will do.

Trust is the cornerstone of Connection and Influence. ***No Trust, No Connection. No Trust, No Influence.***

Greater connection and influence comes from how successfully, creatively - *and positively* - we use what we know about who we know. The more we know about someone in our network, the more ways we can find ways to Be Progress in his or her life.

What are they going for in life?

What do they like?

What are their interests?

Find ways to help them progress based on their needs – not on your services. People want to be in relationships with people who bring progress to their lives.

There must be benefits from the relationship, or it's really no relationship at all.
As the relationship blossoms, continue to look for ways to establish yourself as progress.

The Six Ps of Progress:

Pleasure
Peace of Mind
Profit
Power
Prestige
Pain Avoidance

The 24-Hour NEXT STEP

Get that second progress-based impression in quick. Follow up by text message, e-mail, snail mail, or phone within 24 hours. You want to get the second progress-based impression in quick to build on the momentum of the first. Act on the Next Step you discovered as the next best ways you can Be Progress.

.

Consider going to networking functions with the goal of developing a 'To Do' List of action steps you are going to take within 24 hours on behalf of the people you just connected with.

The longer you wait, the harder it is and the more likelihood that the buzz of meeting you will have waned. Include in your follow-up something specific to the conversation you had with the contact, some way you can Be Progress.

Most people do not follow up because they have nothing to say that builds on the conversation – ***because there was no real conversation!*** They did not learn anything that they can use to build on.

A good follow-up that builds on the first conversation and offers progress sets you apart from the rest. It is strategic communication that begins to solidify your relationship.

Want to really make a Rocking Progress-Based Second Impression?

Actually MAIL a personalized and helpful note as a solid way to make a progress-based second impression. Short, upbeat, and handwritten is ideal - *as long as your writing is legible.* Many feel that a follow-up written thank-you note is better than a follow-up e-mail.

A real signature in ink on real notepaper may take a couple of days to get to them, but in this hyper-digital age, it has the potential of being much more powerful and memorable than an e-mail or digital follow-up.

Again, begin with a compliment, helpful insight or a statement that refers back to the conversation you shared. Keep the tone upbeat. If appropriate:
It could end by suggesting that the two of you
get together for breakfast or lunch.

To reach the 24-hour NEXT STEP Follow-up deadline: Try taking some thank-you stationery or note cards with stamps to business networking events. Write, address, and mail the personalized and helpful notes directly following the event to the people you just made a connection with.

"Make yourself necessary to the world and mankind will give you bread."
-- *Ralph Waldo Emerson*

Reach Out, Forge Ahead!!

Progress Agents don't get stuck in the *"Woulda, Coulda, Shoulda"* Trap. Influence and connection skills are good to possess but they are only useful if we USE them. ***Don't just plan to make connections. Reach out, Forge Ahead!!***

Making connections takes personal self-discipline and dedication. Every day, hundreds of thousands of people have hundreds of thousands of ideas, goals, and intentions – ***but they never take that first step.***

Whenever you ask someone's opinion to help you make an informed decision, even if it is just to find a good sushi bar or something to binge watch, **you are reaping the benefits of influence and connection.**

Gathering new contacts and opening avenues of opportunity increases the number of people in your network. Hey, you've known networking is a good business practice for a while now.

So why have you not made more connections up to this point? One of the main reasons people don't take the first step is they have little vision of the outcome they're looking for through influence and connection. Increase your determination to make new connections by listing the reasons you haven't done more in the past.

It may feel like a safe place, but it is dangerous to live in denial.

Getting to the bottom of your resistances will encourage you to blast through them – *by just doing it.* And once you get on a roll, you won't stop. It could even become second nature to you.

Get out more often. If you don't make connecting with new people a priority, our influence - along with our network - will shrink, stagnate, and lose its strength.

Yes, many networking events happen in the mornings, during lunches, and after hours. **Success is rarely created working 9 to 5.**

Create Strong Belief in Self and Service
Open Face-to-Face Relationships
Deliver Solid First Impressions
Earn Trust
Be Confident.
Make Connections, Get Out and About.
Listen. Expect the Best.
Get Curious, Be Interested.
Give a Hoot.
Display a Pro-Active *Be Progress* Attitude.
(This just in: Your attitude counts for more than your knowledge.)
Be helpful. Get Involved.
Reach Out, Be Optimistic.
Forge Ahead and Don't Quit!!!

"Making miracles is hard work, most people give up before they happen."
— *Sheryl Crow*

Sure, the business world is challenging.
Sure, it's nerve-racking to deal with customers.
Sure, sales can be tough to come by.
Sure, people are often pressed for time.
Sure, influence and connection are tough in this digital age.

But here is something else I know for sure:

People are influenced by, do business with, as well as help, share information, brainstorm, and give referrals to people they trust and value. They trust and value people who have made a real connection and shown they genuinely care about them and are progress for their lives.

Remember:
Progress does not demand perfection, only persistence.

Remember:
Change is inevitable,
Progress is a Choice.

Remember:
Progress is a step forward.
Take today's step.

Be Progress.

About the Author:

Dean Lindsay is the President of The Progress Agents LLC, an education company dedicated to *Empowering Progress in Sales, Service and Workplace Culture.* He is the Host of *The DEAN's List* on the C-Suite TV Network, and has been hailed as an 'outstanding thought leader on the subject of building priceless business relationships' by *Sales and Marketing Executives International* as well as:

- ✓ 'America's Progress Agent' by *The Strategic HR Forum,*
- ✓ 'The Dean of Sales and Service' by *Business Class News,*
- ✓ a 'Sales and Networking Guru' by the *Dallas Business Journal,* and
- ✓ an 'Outstanding Speaker' by the *International Association of Speakers Bureaus.*

Dean is a dynamic international keynote speaker and has had the privilege of sharing his profitable business growth and workplace culture insights in countries across the globe including: *Spain, Turkey, Poland, Ecuador, Mexico, Canada, Venezuela, Sweden and the islands of Aruba and Jamaica.*

Dean's national and international clients include the *United States Patent and Trademark Office, Marriott, American Airlines, Texas A&M, New York Life, Verizon, Aramark Canada, Precision Tune Auto Care, Heinz, House of Blues, Pacific Life & Annuity, Hilton, FASTSIGNS, American Express, Western Union, Nestle, Gold's Gym, Bell Partners, EKOS(Ecuador), ConocoPhillips, Haggar Clothing, and the United States Peace Corp.*

He is a lifetime member of the *Viktor Frankl Institute of Logotherapy,* a cum laude graduate of the *University of North Texas* and served as Guest Lecturer to *UCLA Anderson School of Management* as well as the *International Call Management Institute.*

Continued...

Dean has been a featured contributor to *CEO World Magazine*, *The Smart Manager* (India), *Business Class News, Sales and Service Excellence*, *Training Magazine Europe*, and the American Management Association's *Moving Ahead* magazine. His business views have been featured on *Voice of America* radio and *Monster.com*.

Dean's books have sold over 100,000 copies worldwide and have been translated into *Chinese, Hindi, Polish, Korean, Spanish and Greek.* His books have also been endorsed by a who's who of international business thought leaders including Michael Port (author of *Book Yourself Solid*), Ken Blanchard (author of *The One Minute Manager*), Brian Tracy (author of *The Psychology of Selling*) and Jay Conrad Levinson, the legendary Father of *Guerrilla Marketing*, who calls Dean *'a Master of Progress.'*

Some other stuff… Dean is an award-winning songwriter, a marathon runner, a founding member of the *Texas Shakespeare Festival*, and an alumnus of *Up With People*, the legendary international educational organization with the mission of inspiring young people to make a positive difference in their world.

A couple bits of trivia: Way back in the mid 90's:

✓ Dean served as On-Set Performance Coach to *Grammy* Award Winner LeAnn Rimes on both a *Hallmark Movie of the Week* and on the soap opera *Days of Our Lives.*

✓ Dean was cast as one of the 'Bad Guys' in the Warner Brothers' blockbuster *TWISTER* (*Dean urges you to not look to hard for him in the film however, sharing that 'the flying cow ended up with a bigger part than I did."*).

Dean, his wife Lena, and their two smart, strong and beautiful daughters, Sofia & Ella, live in Plano, Texas.

Endorsements for the Work of Dean Lindsay

"Dean *brings a great sense of how to connect quickly* with people through impactful and fun stories, *I highly recommend Dean*."

— Jim Snow, President,
Gold's Gym International

"Dean was TERRIFIC!!" *– Geri Barton, Director of Customer Service,* ***World Kitchen LLC***

"The *feedback from the attendees was OUTSTANDING*! Dean was humorous, energetic, and very relatable – everyone walked out re-energized too!! We would highly recommend Dean for any event and plan to have him back soon."

— Greg Pressly, Vice President of Customer Operations, ***MetroPCS***

"We had Dean speak at our international Business Partner Conference in Stockholm, Sweden. Dean delivered a very energetic, dynamic and humorous motivational speech for our international Group of reselling partners, focusing on change and progress. I can highly recommend him."

– Sofia Löfblad,
Marketing Director at ***Handheld GroupAB***
(Stockholm, Sweden)

"*Our company hired a keynote speaker but got a life-long business partner and resource for our team*!"

— David Webster, CEO,
Electrical Components International

For Booking Information, visit:
DeanLindsay.com *or call:* ***214-457-5656***

Praise for Dean Lindsay's ***How to Achieve Big PHAT Goals***

"Big PHAT Goals is an extremely helpful book for achieving your personal and professional goals."

— Frank Shankwitz, The Creator and
A Founder of the ***Make-A-Wish Foundation***

"I love, love, love this book! As someone who has been dedicated to setting and achieving personal and team goals for the past 30 years, Big PHAT Goals took my understanding to the next level. I rewrote my goals within days of reading the book, following Dean's formula, and I am already experiencing even greater progress! This is a must read for you, as well as those you lead... and those you love!"

— Catherine Monson, CEO,
FASTSIGNS International, Inc.

"... all the best parts of goal achievement knowledge is collated into one powerful little book. ... The lessons are scale able, practical and edgy. This is a must have addition for every bookshelf."

– ***Everyday Manager.com***

"**...a simple yet highly effective and easy read to help anyone reach higher levels in their personal and professional life! I highly recommend it!"**

– Larry North, Legendary Fitness Expert &
Author of ***Living Lean, Get Fit! & Slim Down For Life***

Dean Lindsay's Customizable Keynote, Workshop & Coaching Programs Designed to Help Empower Progress in Sales, Service and Workplace Culture include:

- **Celebrating Service Excellence:**
  ***Rock the Customer Experience**
  Featuring the Cherishing Customers CARE Model & ForWORDs & BackWORDS:
  Words & Phrases That MOVE Business Communication

- **Becoming a Progress Agent!:**
  Keys to INFLUENCE & CONNECTION

- **Cracking The CONNECTION CODE:**
  ***CODE Prospecting** & *4 Steps to Priceless Business Relationships*

- **Welcoming the Rise of Progress Leadership:**
  ****Change Management is Dead!***

- **How to Achieve Big PHAT Goals:**
  Goal Alignment leads to Employee Engagement
  *- Have a Big PHAT **Sales** Year!*
  *- How to Achieve Big PHAT **Team** Goals*

- **The PROGRESS Challenge:**
  Working & Winning in a World of Change

- **Be a BAM!:**
  *Keys to Becoming a **B**usiness **A**ttraction **M**agnet*

Please visit: **DeanLindsay.com**
for more information.

Connect with ***Dean Lindsay on Social Media:***

YouTube Channel: **DeanLindsay**

Join our Facebook Group: **The Progress Agents**

Facebook: **@DeanLindsayProgressAgent**

Twitter: **@DeanLindsay**

LinkedIn: **@Dean Lindsay**

Instagram: **@DeanoLindsay**

Email: **Dean@DeanLindsay.com**

Website: **DeanLindsay.com**

Visit **DeanLindsay.com** or call **214-457-5656** for ***Discount Bulk Pricing*** on a variety of Progress Agent Educational Materials including:

- ✓ **The Progress Agent Handbook For Influence and Connection**
- ✓ **How to Achieve Big PHAT Goals**
- ✓ **Diving for Referral Pearls (CD)**
- ✓ **DISC Behavioral Assessment Profiles**